ALASKA TRACKS

A collection of life stories as told by
Alaskan hunters, fishermen and trappers.

RANDY ZARNKE

ISBN 978-1-59433-398-9

Library of Congress Catalog Card Number: 2013940672

Copyright 2013 Randy Zarnke
—First Printing July 2013 —
—Second Printing September 2013 —
—Third Printing April 2014—
—Fourth Printing December 2014—
—Fifth Printing November 2016—

All rights reserved, including the right of
reproduction in any form, or by any mechanical
or electronic means including photocopying or
recording, or by any information storage or
retrieval system, in whole or in part in any
form, and in any case not without the
written permission of the author and publisher.

Manufactured in the United States of America.

PO Box 221974 Anchorage, Alaska 99522-1974
books@publicationconsultants.com—www.publicationconsultants.com

Foreword

"RESPECT FOR THE PAST-COMMITMENT TO THE FUTURE"

The history of the fur trade is inseparable from the history of Canada and the United States. Explorers quickly recognized the economic advantages of the export of fur pelts to Europe and began the trade that would define the location of major cities in both countries, first as fur trading posts and much later as modern metropolises. North American Fur Auction's trading activities date back to the foundation of the Hudson's Bay Company (HBC) in 1670. From the earliest days, the marketing of furs was done in a competitive environment, originally by a sealed bid and subsequently at public auctions held in London, England.

In February 1987, the Hudson's Bay Company sold their Canadian fur auction business to the Canadian Fur Division management group and its supporting fur producer groups to continue the 300-year tradition of Hudson's Bay in the fur trade. In June 1989, the new company purchased Hudson's Bay Company's New York auction business. The Company changed its name in 1992 to North American Fur Producers Marketing Inc. and the combined auction activities of the two companies have since been conducted under the trade name "North American Fur Auctions."

North American Fur Auctions is the largest wild fur auction house in the world. As a leader in the industry, we have invested heavily in developing new markets as well as maintaining traditional markets for wild fur. Our outstanding assortments, large buyer attendances and extensive promotional work in all the major international fur markets benefit our shippers by providing them with the highest possible price for their product.

In the Fall of 1996, NAFA established the Wild Fur Shippers Council (NAWFSC) to enhance the working relationship between the company and our wild fur producers. The Wild Fur Shippers Council gives trappers a strong voice in NAFA's operations. We've described our relationship with trappers as a partnership. The Wild Fur Shippers Council is a meaningful way of making that partnership even stronger.

On May 2, 2000, exactly 330 years after the issuing of the Charter of Incorporation for the original Hudson's Bay Company, the NAFA Wild Fur Shippers Council, representing the ownership interest of Canadian and American trappers, completed the circle with the purchase of shares in NAFA. This historic step ensured trappers that they would always have an aggressive, professional marketing agency to sell and promote their fur.

North American Fur Auctions and The North American Wild Fur Shippers Council are proud to sponsor this book documenting the history of trapping in Alaska. The NAWFSC has a membership of wild fur producers throughout North America. We are committed to preserving and promoting the culture, heritage and economic viability of fur harvesting. With the sponsorship of this book, we believe that the rich history of the Alaska outdoors and the memories of veteran outdoorsmen will be preserved for future generations to enjoy.

North American Fur Auctions   **Wild Fur Shippers Council**

THIS ORAL HISTORY PROJECT WAS SUPPORTED BY:

of Alaska

....

I wish to acknowledge the financial support of:

The Outdoor Heritage Foundation of Alaska, ConocoPhillips, The Alaska Furbearer Management Council, Usibelli Coal Mine, Era Aviation, North American Fur Auctions, and Wild Fur Shippers Council.

Without their support, this project would not have been possible. Each helped in their own way. All helped make the project a success.

I also wish to thank:

Joan O'Leary who transcribed most of the interviews, John Majak who shared the wonderful sketches found throughout the book, Libbie Martin who edited the manuscript and offered much-needed advice, and Ryan Ragan who handled design and lay-out of this book. I appreciate the special skills you brought to this project. It was my pleasure working with you.

—RANDY ZARNKE

THIS BOOK IS DEDICATED TO THE MEMORY OF:

- Alaska trapper Dean Wilson, who led by quiet example.

- Alaska trapper Paul Kirsteatter, who inspired many by his accomplishments and stories of days gone by.

- My Father Marty, who helped me learn to love the outdoors as much as he did.

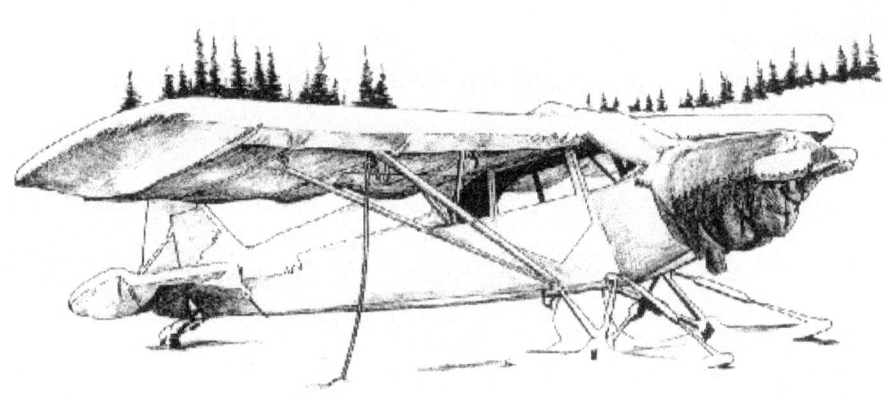

Published by the Alaska Trappers Association - 2013
Printing and binding by Publication Consultants

INTRODUCTION

This book is based upon a project to record "oral history" interviews with veteran outdoorsmen and –women around the state of Alaska. The primary purpose of this project is to preserve the memories of people who have lived an active outdoor lifestyle. The secondary purpose is to share those memories with interested individuals. This book will be one means of accomplishing that secondary objective.

The project has taken me from Ketchikan to Kotzebue and Tok to Dillingham. At the time of this writing, we have 171 interviews in the collection. Obviously, not all of those people could be included in this book. I've purposely selected interviews with a wide geographic distribution. I believe there is value in sharing both the similarities and differences of outdoor activities from different areas of the State.

You'll find relatively few words of mine in this book. With the exception of the introductions and transitions, the words are almost entirely those spoken by the person whose name appears on the first page of each chapter. I've intentionally refrained from wholesale re-writing of each interview. I firmly believe that readers will find this direct personal flavor to be the most appealing aspect of this book.

This project has been both enjoyable and rewarding. I've met some of the finest people on the face of this earth. Regardless of community status or business accomplishments or financial wealth, these folks recognize that their fondest memories are of the times they spent hunting, fishing and trapping The Great Land. I hope that you enjoy their stories.

—RANDY ZARNKE

> *Full-length audio interviews ranging in length from 30 to 80 minutes are available. You can listen to the unique vocal flavorings of the characters in this book as well as many other Alaskans. More information is available online at: www.alaskatrappers.org. Click on "oral history interviews."*

Contents:

Southern Southeast

Bruce Johnstone 3
Earl Callihan 9
Duke Short 13
Ben Forbes 18

Northern Southeast

Ken Fanning 25
Adam Greenwald 31
Alf Skaflestad 39

South-Central

Red Beeman 45
Larry Kritchen 49
June Moore 60
Marlin Grasser 68

Eastern Interior

Richard Carroll 77
LeNora Conkle 83
Tor Holmboe 88
Paul Kirsteatter 96
Dean Wilson 103

Northwest

Bill Fickus 111
Bob Uhl 118
Daniel Karmun 125

Central & Western Interior

Richard Frank 133
Susie Charlie 141
Al Wright 147
Ron Long 160
Ken Deardorff 168

Kodiak & Bristol Bay

Darrell Farmen 176
Norm Sutliff 181
John Nicholson 187

Kenai Peninsula

Will Troyer 194
Lyle Garner 202
Jim Rearden 208

About the Author 217

VII

Southern Southeast

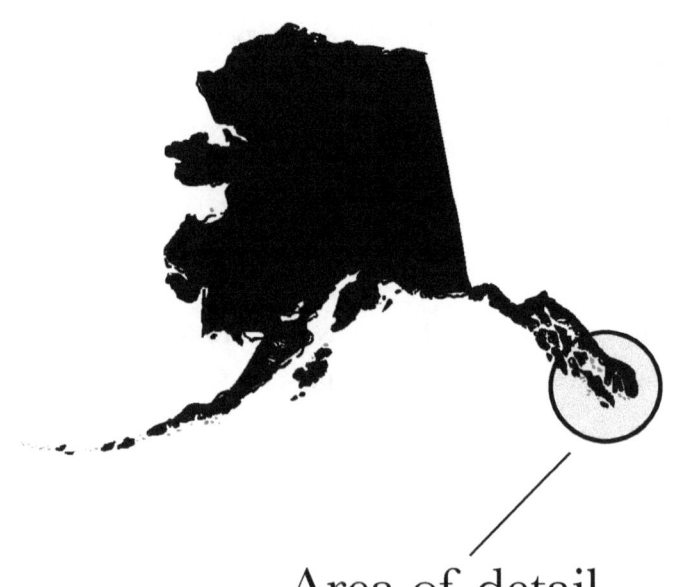

Area of detail

Petersburg, Sitka, Ketchikan, Kake

BRUCE JOHNSTONE

Ketchikan, AK

Merely surviving was a challenge for many Alaska families in the early 1900s. Bruce Johnstone's father became ill during the 1918 Spanish Flu pandemic. With his father disabled, Bruce became the family's provider. To earn money Bruce took up bear hunting. Bears are dangerous, even for adults. Imagine how challenging it must have been for a boy.

In the early days, there wasn't much to do up here for money. In the summer-time, we had logging and in winter-time, we would trap. We depended on deer meat for our families.

From the time I was about ten years old, I had to make a living for the whole family. The Smithsonian had been paying my brother $45 a piece for black bear skulls and $75 for grizzlies. If I could get one bear a month, that was pretty good money. I'd sell the feet to the Chinese, and I got seven dollars apiece for the galls. So, if you add it all up, one bear would bring in quite a bit of money. Most of my bear hunting was up around Admiralty, Baranof and

Chichagof Islands. Back when I was hunting bears, I didn't guide for them.

My worst scare came in the winter of 1922-23. I was trapping at the head of Roger's Bay over on the mainland. Back in those days, we didn't have game laws like we do nowadays. We started trapping when we thought the fur was prime. All I had for a gun in those days was a single-shot 12-gauge shotgun with a broken extractor. I had a piece of lead that would just fit down the barrel. I would drop it in there to knock the shells out.

One day, I hadn't shot the gun and I didn't want to drop the lead through while it was in the house. I left the gun in the skiff. The next day I went out and it was raining hard. The barrel was half full of water and I poured it out. I didn't see any ducks that day, so I had no reason to shoot the gun and forgot about the old shell in the chamber. I went into the woods to look at the traps I set the day before. I walked up to a set and there was a cub bear in the trap. I was wondering what to do with it. I heard a noise and the mother was coming up behind me. I thought about the old gun then … whether it would fire or not.

I was a runt. Shooting a 12-gauge would cause me to take a few steps backwards. I knew I had only one shot. I got down on my knees so I would be level with the bear and expecting it to rear up. Instead, it walked almost into the end of a gun. I pulled the trigger, the hammer went down, there was a click … and then it fired. The bear was dead. That was the scariest thing that ever happened to me.

Trapping was a reliable source of income for Johnstone and other men in Alaska back in the early 1900s. He's trapped most of the furbearers in Southeast Alaska, and saw first-hand how nature adapts.

In the early days, they didn't use traps at all. They had a three-inch auger and bored a hole in a tree. Then drive some nails in at an angle and put the bait in the back. When either a marten or mink would stick their head in, they couldn't get out.

In those days, if you caught ten marten in a season that was a big year. Now, some of these people catch 200 marten in a season. You can use most anything for bait, but seal meat is the best. Fish or ducks are good, too.

When I first started trapping, I only had a small boat. It wasn't big enough to sleep aboard. We would fall a red cedar and split out shakes to make a shack to live in while trapping.

Back in 1933, I stocked Prince of Wales with marten. We trapped them off the mainland and took them over. They didn't allow trapping until the war was over in 1945.

They were big and almost yellow in color. Now the marten on Prince of Wales are all dark. The marten up on Kuiu Island are almost golden color. The furbuyers really liked them. When we were getting $40 for ordinary colors, it was $80 for the golden.

Later in the season, I would go after mink. I would trap marten at the head of the bays early in the season and move out later for mink and otter. All my mink sets were trail sets. Up in the Interior, they use bait, but down here there are big mink trails along the beach. When I started trapping, I only caught 15 to 20 mink per season. As I got better, I brought that up to 75 to 80 per season.

In one sense, otter are like beaver. The hides are mighty hard to take care of. You can catch a beaver in every set if you are in good beaver country, but a beaver is hard to skin and stretch. You didn't want to put out too many sets because you didn't want to get too many at a time. So three beaver sets is as many as I'd make in a day.

The most I averaged for mink was about $30. Beaver went as high as $80. One year, we got $20 straight for otter and the next year they went for as high as $120.

I don't know why people are against trapping. There was an article in the newspaper this morning. Somebody found a dead rat in the street. The animal rights people are making a big stink about it ... when a rat dies!! People have gone crazy.

Bruce spent many years guiding hunters for the region's giant brown bears. He met many interesting people.

I didn't start guiding until 1923 and 1924. I didn't get a license until 1936. When I first started the guiding, I was guiding the guides around, the people that wanted to get licenses. I guided for close to 40 years.

I guided for Campbell Church, Jr. He used to have a bunch of boats up here every year. I never did outfit anything for myself. I would take three parties per year, mostly spring and fall hunts. There were six to eight hunters at a time. Each hunt would last about 30 days.

During the Great Depression of 1929, many of the millionaires just closed shop and went hunting. They had plenty of money. The Mellon family from Pittsburgh would come up every five years for a hunt. At that time, they were the wealthiest family in the United States.

I arrested one of the Mellons; took him into Juneau because he shot an extra bear. The skipper of the boat and I got together and took him to the game warden, Homer Jewel. He got a big kick out of that!

Bruce came up against some overzealous game wardens. Most of the time, the situations were resolved to the hunter's satisfaction.

One year in the middle of February, my brother and I were logging down at Boca de Quadra. This was back before World War II. They broke the tail shaft in their boat motor. My brother was going to row to town to get help. We shot a goat and hung it up in front of the cabin and didn't think anything about it. The game law says you can take animals for survival. The game warden came by and we flagged him down. He cited us for killing a goat out of season. The judge told me if we all pled guilty we could get right out. If we didn't, he'd have to hold a trial. We all pled guilty, he fined us $25, and I lost my guide license. When I got out of the service, I wrote to Juneau to get my license back. The Commissioner came down and wanted to know how I lost it.

I told him, "Go over to the machine shop and they'll tell you the whole story. How we broke down and the game warden towed us to the shop and the machinist put in the new tail shaft."

The Commissioner talked to him. When he came back he said, "You'll get your license back. What do you think we should do with the game warden?"

I said, "The best thing to do is get rid of him."

He went back to Juneau. About ten days later he came down to have a talk with the Trappers Association. They fired the warden.

Hunting Alaska's wild game isn't easy or safe. Bruce has his share of bear stories, including the time he was seriously mauled by three grizzlies. Since he survived, the story has a happy – and humorous – ending.

I tangled with a bear up on the Unuk River in 1958. I went moose hunting with two other fellows. We went up two days before the season to make camp and do a little trout fishing. The next day we went back to get more trout. Where we gutted the fish, the bear had licked the blood off of the rocks. The next day, I went to get some ducks for camp meat. I had a light-weight Ithaca shotgun back then.

I had three shells in the gun when I saw these three bear. I made a lot of noise, I didn't want no bear. They came through the scattered willows; a great big boar, a female, and a two year old. I saw they meant business. I thought I'd take the biggest one first. I was going to shoot the boar under the ear. Just as I pulled the trigger, the female hit me and I shot his eyes out. He went down, but I didn't kill him. He was making a lot of noise.

The female stood up right in front of me. I stuck the gun up under her chin, but the gun wouldn't fire. She picked me up by the back of my leg and shook me and everything tore out. She went up by the boar for a little while, but pretty soon she come over the bank to me. I was laying next to a muddy glacier stream. I was trying to feel for the shotgun. She knocked me down and started biting on me again. She went back by the boar. By that time, I had the gun up, but it was full of water. I dumped out the water. When she come over the bank, I pulled the trigger and that one fired. It hit just a little behind the ear.

By that time, the little fellow got into it. I had one shell left and I could hear a boat coming. It was a guide with three hunters. He was an old-timer in this area, one of our good guides. He ran the boat up through the tall grass to where I was. The cub and I were rolling around fighting. He shot two times and missed both of us. The next shot hit the bear in the foot and that made him mad. Then the old-timer shot one more time and killed the bear.

They took me out to where the boat was anchored and one of the hunters was going to do the doctoring. They rolled me over on the floor and pulled my pants off.

The fellow who was going to be the doc says, "If we only had a bottle of hootch here, we could pour that in the holes and stop the infection."

The skipper was a Seventh Day Adventist. He said, "I don't allow no booze on my boat."

One of the other hunters says, "I smuggled some aboard!"

He brought up the bottle, poured a glass half-full and handed it to the guy who was going to do the doctoring. Instead of giving it to me, he drank it himself. Then he poured the rest of that whiskey into those holes. I think it done the trick. I never had any infections at all. That year, there were very few berries and very few fish. I think those bears were starving to death.

{BRUCE JOHNSTONE PASSED AWAY IN 2006}

Ketchikan, AK. circa 1900s.

EARL CALLIHAN
Petersburg, AK

Earl Callihan looks the part of the classic sourdough. His face is ruddy from years spent out in the weather. His hair and beard are white as snow. Earl prefers wool pants with red suspenders. Most importantly, he still has a twinkle in his eye which reflects the wonderful life that he's led. Earl grew up in the lumber towns of Idaho. He gravitated to the lumber industry of Southeast Alaska. During the winters, he lived a bare-bones existence on a boat. Food was always close at hand ... marine life from the ocean or deer from the land. In this first segment from Earl's interview, he describes how he landed a prime job as a teenager during the Great Depression.

I started working in the woods in Priest Lake, Idaho. Walker Brothers was the name of the outfit. One of the truck drivers, had some woman problems in Washington. He left to get that straightened out and he never did come back!

Stanton Walker said, "Let's take The Kid and make a 'double clutcher' outta him!" I didn't know s*** from wild honey back then! By gosh, I rode with Stanton on a trip or two and then I started hauling logs on my own. They were big logging trucks in them days. Old gas engine Internationals. Three thousand feet of logs was a big load. The roads were so bad you couldn't haul more than that. You'd sink, truck and all.

Then one day along comes Stanton's dad. He was the head of the lumber company. He says to me, "I know your folks, Burt and Alice, real well. Why aren't you in school?" I says, "I got to work. Heck I got a job here and there isn't another job in the country! I want to stay and work for you." He says, "No, you got to go to school." He come down to the bunkhouse that night and he told me, "You either go to school or I'll fire you." I didn't know what to do! I was a kid. What would you do?

When I finished school and came back, they had bought three or four brand spanking new Diamond T diesels. Them was real good trucks in them days. That would be in 1938! Punkin'rollin' kid like me getting right in a new Diamond T diesel!!

I had that in my shirt pocket when I come to Alaska. I had already served my apprenticeship in the woods on them logging trucks in Idaho. So it was no problem for me to get a job here. In fact I drove for Valentine Logging Company on Admiralty Island for the bigger part of 25 years in the summer-time. In the winter-time when the camp was down, you'd do nothing. It would give you the chance to hunt and trap all you wanted to. It worked out pretty good like that.

In this next section, Earl relates an encounter with one of the giant coastal brown bears of Southeast Alaska. It started and ended on a positive note. However, there were a few tense moments in between.

I never had any real close encounters. Been a little concerned a time or two. There was only one time I was real scared, but it turned out alright.

I was where the tide comes in to a salt chuck lagoon. There was a good deer crossing. When the tide was out they would cross without ever getting their feet wet. I thought maybe I'd down a deer if one came by. It was evening, and I hadn't seen a thing. I turned to leave. I had a skiff down the beach a little ways, tied to a tree there. I walked down that way and by gosh this bear come out of the brush. It wasn't no great big danger at all. A bear that's 100 or 200 yards from you is no threat. I didn't pay much attention to him at first. However, I noticed that he seen me and I could tell by the way he was watching that he was interested in what he was seeing. And that son of a gun, he just deliberately come right down to where the tide come in and washed the rocks almost clean. He stopped and stood up on his hind feet a second or two and I thought I'd discourage him! I just set down on one knee. I was real careful that I shot a foot or two on one side of him in them rocks there. I turned one loose. I thought he'd just drop to his feet and run like a deer. There was no other thought in my mind at all. BANG! Off went that H&H and just instantly he dropped to his feet and come like a race horse to where I was. Pulled up about 20 yards away, and stopped!

Well, you know, I was a little concerned but I didn't want to kill him. I was talking to him and I told him, "You SOB! You make one more move and I'll kill you. I've got just the equipment to do it with right here; .375 H&H." Feed him one of those 350 grain pills! That's big enough to discourage a bear. That's the reason I carried that old rifle. You know, I'm sure he didn't know what I was talking about and maybe he didn't even hear me. He walked around there a little bit. My palms were so sweaty that I thought the rifle would slip out of my hands. He pooped around a little bit and went up on the beach and took a mouth full of old dry grass. When he did that I knew that whatever he had in mind, he changed his mind. He walked down the beach a little ways. I went and got the skiff and carried on.

That was the closest to having one deliberately charge! He didn't just 'happen' to run in my direction. He knew exactly what he was doing! He might have been an old one because he was a lighter brown and he was almost grey in some places. I'm sure I never seen him anymore. There was a time not too long ago, I recognized most of those bears. That was the only time I had seen that one. He don't know how close he came to getting a 350 grain hard-nosed Hornaday right between the 'cook house' and the 'bunk house.'

Earl has fond memories of many of the men he worked with over the years. In this next segment, Earl describes a harrowing accident that befell one of his close friends. The episode concludes with a humorous alternative to the true story.

A friend of mine, Merle Passenger, was an engineer on a light house tender. He was a good story teller. He was a BS'er from way back! He'd tell you a story you knew was a lie but you were damn near tempted to believe him anyway!

Merle had the awfulest looking arm that you had ever seen. Horrible looking thing. Scars! You just couldn't imagine! Nobody had an arm that looked any worse than Merle Passenger's arm.

What happened ... they was 'barring over' an old gas engine in one of the cannery light-house tenders. There's holes around the perimeter of the fly wheel. In order to start the engine, you stick a bar in one of them holes and push that fly wheel over until it's in a firing position. Something went 'gunny sack.' The engine hiccupped and backfired. They still had the bar in the fly wheel. That bar went over and hit Merle in the arm. Just shattered it.

Jiminy Christ, it was a terrible looking thing! There was no medical treatment available. They just put it back together the best way they could and wrapped something around it to hold it together. It just healed up like that.

I've heard Merle tell a slightly different story, too. Him and another guy wintered in Taku harbor and they could see some goats up on the hills. They decided they would go up there and get a goat. He was saying how tough that goat was. He said we tried to bake it, fry it, boil it, that doggone goat was so tough. They eventually decided to grind it in the meat grinder. According to Merle's version, the meat grinder backfired and it hit him in the arm. That's how his arm got in such a hell of a shape. The meat grinder back fired! Now that's a tough goat!

{EARL CALLIHAN PASSED AWAY IN 2006}

DUKE SHORT
Kake, AK

Duke Short's family moved to the cannery at Tyee in 1946, when Duke was just a boy. His lifetime of hunting, fishing and trapping in the surrounding area has provided many fond memories.

Tyee was founded as a whaling station in 1907. They shut down in 1913. I don't know if it was due to a lack of whales. I think petroleum oil was coming in and the whale oil was going out. A family named Green bought it and started a salmon cannery. It was a family-run outfit. They had seven fish traps ... made of big spruce logs. The first head log was probably 75 feet long -- that was the base of the trap. There were also side logs and jigger corners. The logs were spliced with bolts that were six, seven feet long. We also lashed the logs together with 7/8-inch cable.

One guy was designated as the wire foreman. They made up big rolls of wire and loaded them on a scow. When the tide would come in, they'd take the scow out to the trap frame and attach the rolls of wire to the frame.

When I was a kid, I ran a small cannery tender. I'd move the scow around where the wire boss would tell me and they would roll these bundles off into the water.

I always thought setting traps was kind of fun because you got away from the cannery. You lived right on the rigging scow and you always had a good cook. When you are young, you like to eat pretty good.

The resident deer population provided an ample supply of red meat for the Short family. Duke and his brother also harvested deer for local elders.

Most of the time we didn't have any trouble getting deer. We would go early up above timberline. That was a hell of a climb up there, but in those days we didn't mind it too much. There were herds of deer up there. You could look out and see 20 or 30 deer in an area. Our family (my mom and dad and brothers) ate about 30 deer a year. Tyee was wonderful deer country.

The old Norwegian fishermen would fish when the weather was good and when they wanted to. They didn't worry about having a lot of money. About the only thing they worried about was having enough to eat. They couldn't get out hunting any more, so me and my brother would shoot deer for them. We'd bring them a deer and they would get together and play cribbage and can deer meat. When you get older, you think about the good old days and those are the kinds of things that I think about.

Bounty hunting was a reliable source of money for a young man with an accurate rifle. This practice is long gone, but not forgotten.

I hunted eagles for bounty years ago. If you tell people that now, they think you're really a bad person. We got two bucks apiece for eagles. The biggest day I had was during a herring run. The eagles were eating the herring and I killed 33 eagles. The only reason I didn't get more was I run out of bullets.

We hunted seal for bounty, too. We shot at quite a distance sometimes.

When you shoot from 250, 300 yards, you need a good steady rest. I never had a lot of success shooting out of a skiff.

Like most people who spend time outdoors in Southeast Alaska, Duke has stories of encountering the big brown bears for which the region is famous.

Every kid wants to kill a big brown bear. When we first came up here, we killed a couple of bears and then we didn't think much about it any more. We killed some that had to be killed. We had bears jump us a few times and we had to lay them down, but we didn't actually hunt for them any more.

One time back in '47, our whole family was walking from home over to the cannery. I was ahead and mom was behind me. Dad and my brother was behind us. A bear started coming for us. I seen it come out of this bed and I shot. I couldn't see any affect and I shot again. I thought I was missing. My last shot hit it in the head and it fell right at my feet. We were pretty excited. I turned to my Mom and said, "That damn thing charged us." She said, "No he didn't charge. He wasn't on his hind feet." She had it in her head a bear had to be on its hind feet to charge. I don't know where that came from.

Another time, me and my brother were hunting deer at Point Bartlett. I had a .357 Roberts with a 10-power scope. We all hand-loaded our ammunition in those days. I had some shells that were kind of sticky in the chamber. I was planning to just shoot them off. I heard something and here come a brown bear through the water. I would have let him go but he was coming right for me. I pulled up and shot. The first shot hit him in the chest cavity. The next shot hit him in the same spot on the other side.

I had a German Shepherd dog with me. The dog attacked him and they run by me maybe seven, eight feet away. When they went past, I shot him through the ribs. I think that was the first time the bear saw me. He came toward me. I jammed the gun right against his chest as he jumped and pulled the trigger. I kept backing up and he kept coming. I hauled off and hit him in the head with the gun. I was pretty strong in those days. The only thing it did was knock me down. I was laying in the water with what was left of the gun. I had forgotten about my brother Wayne. Pretty soon "WHOMP," a bunch of blood and water hit me in the face. I just sat there and then "BOOM" again and again. Wayne heard the ruckus and came to help. I shot [the bear] four times with that little 87 grain bullet, but they didn't do much. Wayne had a .30-06, and that finished him off.

The Short family lived off the bounty of the land and sea. Even for them, some money was necessary. Trapping provided another means to supplement the family income.

My brother and dad trapped. After two or three years, I started trapping, too. We heard stories about all the money trappers made. Unfortunately, we didn't make all that money. We made a little spare money trapping is about all I can say. I think 1959 was probably our best year. We caught about 350 mink and 40 otter.

There was a furbuyer here in Kake named Ernest Kirberger. He was an old German, but he could speak fluent Tlingit. When I was running the mail boat, he would travel with me. That mail run was about 800 miles and had 33 stops. In those days, there was somebody living in just about every bay. He would go ashore at every place and buy fur. He would brag on those furs, "A baby could eat off of them, they are so clean." He'd really make the guy feel good and get the furs as cheap as he could. We thought they paid us a fair price. Most people think they are getting robbed when they sell something and don't get the amount they were hoping for. Fishermen think the same way about not getting enough for their fish.

Duke recalls an interesting episode in Tyee's history.

We had a trapping cabin with a colorful history. It had been a floating scow owned by a couple of whores. It was mostly a house on floats. They also had a boot-legging, home-brew operation and a jukebox on board. They wanted to move to Warm Springs, so they hired some troller to tow them. Half-way there, the two women got drunk and got into an argument. The troller didn't want to deal with them, so he just cut them loose. Another troller came by and towed them into Tyee.

The superintendent at Tyee was named Stefanson. After supper at the cookhouse, Mrs. Stef would get a hold of Stef's arm and they would walk to the steamer dock. One night, here comes the troller towing in this floating whorehouse. Them old gals was drunk and they had that jukebox going and they didn't have many clothes on doing a dance out on the deck. They said Mrs. Stef almost had a heart attack. We really didn't see many airplanes around here in those days, but there was one in the next day and took those women out.

A few years later, we towed that scow over to Warm Springs. We put a stove and bunks in it, and boy it was a comfortable place. We trapped out of it for years.

Short's view of agency personnel and policies has changed over time. He wonders where common sense went.

We never did really have any trouble with the law of any kind. We killed deer out of season every year. There was plenty of deer and people lived remote. Nobody seemed to care in those days and I'm sure the wardens knew about it. They just didn't investigate. Of course, if it was brought to their attention, they'd have to do something.

In those days, if you wanted to build a cabin on the beach, you just built one. The Forest Service didn't know it or didn't say anything. If you wanted a homesite, it was five or ten dollars and you'd get a homesite. Now it is getting so you can't do stuff like that any more. You find you are in trouble.

For example, some friends in Petersburg had cabins and the Forest Service made them have a certain color of green on their roof. One guy didn't have the right shade of green and they got on him for that. I think that is harassment. Another example ... there was a warden I've known ever since he was about six years old. When we were selling a load of halibut, he asked me for a picture identification. I think that is harassment, too. People have to realize rules are only guidelines and you have to use common sense.

{DUKE SHORT PASSED AWAY IN 2012}

BEN FORBES
Sitka, AK

Ben Forbes was born in Wisconsin in 1906. His family moved around searching for a better life. However, it wasn't wanderlust that brought him to Alaska in the 1940s. He can thank Uncle Sam for that.

When I was five years old, we lived on a wheat ranch in Alberta. The gophers are a pest out there. Dad says he's going to put me in business. He bought a single shot Steven's .22 rifle and one box of ammunition. He says, "I'll pay you a penny per tail for gophers you shoot. You've got to put those bullets where they'll do you some good." That was my early training in hunting for money.

When World War II broke out, I was working for the Navy. They sent me up here to Alaska, building air bases. My trip up here was interesting. Everyone was addressing me as a general. I didn't quite understand that. Later on, I looked at my papers. Under the category of "Job Class" they had me listed as "General Foreman." So, to all those guys, I was a General … General Foreman.

We finished up the air base on Annette Island in record time. One day, a patrol came back and one of the planes was doing victory rolls over the field. When he landed, he said he had got a submarine. He told his commanding officer where it was. They sent a patrol boat out, and came back with about 300 pounds of whale blubber. So they immediately had a whale recognition class.

With the war drawing to a close, Ben's skills were no longer needed. He shifted into the civilian sector and created a marine repair business, recycling an unused Navy craft into a mobile shop.

When we chased the Japanese out of the Aleutians, the Navy kinda turned me loose. I told a friend of mine I wanted to go into the marine repair business here in Sitka. He told me the Navy had a float [raft] made out of logs, 90-foot long and 40 feet wide. The Seabees had a warehouse that was 60 feet long and almost wide as the float that I could have for free. We put the building on the float, and I had a floating repair shop. Before that, people had to struggle to get work done on their boat. With my set-up, they could just tie up to the float, with everything right there. It saved them a lot of time.

Ben's mobile repair shop earned him recognition as a man who could get things accomplished. This capability led him in a new lucrative and satisfying, direction. Ben became one of the most well-known and successful bear guides in all of Southeast Alaska.

At that time, there were no bear guides in Sitka. A game warden here in Sitka talked to me about becoming a bear guide.

I said, "Yes, I'm interested, but how can I do it? The law requires three years of acting as an assistant guide."

He said, "I can give you the exam and if you pass it, you'll be a guide."

I took the exam and got 99 out of 100 questions.

Alaska has more lakes, rivers, and wetlands than any other state. To be safe and successful, a Southeast Alaska guide needs a good boat and navigation skills, as well as a working knowledge of the area.

I managed to get a boat that was suitable for charter work. It was a 26-foot Steelcraft. It wasn't the best charter boat, but it served the purpose. We got started hunting bear and deer around here with that. I wanted a better boat, so we went down to Seattle and I found a 32-foot Chriscraft. An independent boat builder down there made some small changes that made it more suitable for up here; more covered corners, bigger fuel tanks, and instead of a propane stove he put a diesel stove in it that provided heat. My last boat was a 44-footer and that was almost ideal.

My boats were all called *Hunter* ... Hunter I, Hunter II, Hunter III, Hunter IV. Then my wife put the brakes on that.

She said, "No more Hunters. This boat doesn't look like a Hunter, and we'll give it a different name. I wanna call it Beautiful Water, but I wanna put it in another language."

So she used Italian, and the boat was named *Aqua Bella*. It had sleeping accommodations for eight, which was another big plus. Sometimes the hunters have their wife, at least most of 'em say it's their wife. Everyone asked for private rooms for each couple, as well as rooms for my assistant guides and myself and my wife. So it worked out pretty good.

Most of the hunting was done with skiffs. I painted 'em grey so they'd blend in with the water. You could drag 'em ashore and the bears wouldn't notice 'em. We'd sit down low in the boat so we weren't very visible. I got ahold of motors that were quiet. At high speeds, they were pretty noisy, but at trolling speeds they were very quiet. We'd just cruise the shoreline 'til we saw a bear and then go ashore some distance away, and come back and stalk.

My wife went along on the trips as cook. I taught her how to start the boat, how to run it, and how to handle the anchor winch. A lot of times, we'd take the skiffs and go hunting with 'em and you want the big boat to follow and pick you up for staying overnight. I could call her on the radio and tell her where we were and how to get there. She'd run the boat down and anchor it, and be there waiting for us.

Bears are a challenge for hunter and guide. Ben admits he went through a learning process.

I had to kind of learn the game a little bit … where to find the bears, how to sneak up on them, and where to shoot them. They're a tough animal. You can wound a bear pretty badly and he's still a very dangerous adversary if he takes a notion to fight. A sow bear is the most dangerous of all, especially if she's got cubs, 'cause she doesn't want you near those cubs. She'll try to get her cubs right close to her and keep 'em there. She's also willing to retreat if she has a chance. I learned if you run into a sow with cubs, you just back off and leave her alone and she'll leave.

A bear's a pretty wary animal. He's got eyesight as good as a man's and his hearing is exceptional, so they're a difficult animal to stalk. If he gets one scent of you, he's gone. And if he hears you or sees you, he doesn't waste much time, either. Once he gets into brush, he's as good as gone.

There's only once I ever got a bear in the brush, and that was a kind of a heart-stopping deal. The hunter shot him at about 12 feet. We followed this bear into the woods, and we were sneaking along. The bear was eating some berries and must have stopped. We were up within 12 feet of him before we realized it. I just put the STOP sign out real quick. I motioned the hunter up alongside of me, and pointed where I knew the bear had to be. When he saw that bear his eyes got real big. He was surprised at seeing it that close. He eventually shot it.

I told all my hunters the game laws up here say that if you wound a bear, you gotta track it down and kill it. So I says, "I wanna make a deal with you. If you shoot the bear and I know you hit it, then I can follow your shot with one of mine. That might save us a lot of problems."

I carried a custom-made rifle. A gunsmith got a .45 caliber barrel and put it on an action, which had a magazine and bolt that were big enough to hold an extra large case. The result was a .450 caliber and I used 500 grain bullets.

I didn't tell my hunters to use a certain caliber. I'd tell 'em what's desirable, but a lot of 'em didn't have that caliber gun. You can kill a bear with a .30-06 if you get 'em in the right place. In fact, I had one guy come up here with a .270 and he killed a bear all right.

I remember one bear hunt we had up in Deep Inlet. The bear breeding season is in the spring. This great big male bear was chasing a really young sow. He wanted to breed her and she didn't want to be bred. He'd catch up with her and try to climb on top of her and she just about disappeared underneath him. Then she'd scramble away and run, and he'd chase her down again. We eventually shot the male. She kept him so busy we were able to get in position where he didn't know we were there. When he went by, we had the chance to knock him off. He squared ten feet.

In the spring, we'd normally take two hunters per trip and three trips. That's six hunters in the spring. In the fall, we'd usually take the same number. So the number of hunters ranged between ten and 12 per year. We were almost always successful. I don't think that we ever went out that we didn't get a bear.

I might have been a little stiff on my prices. When I first started, I charged 'em a thousand dollars to get a bear, plus a hundred dollars a day for room and board on the boat. If they didn't get a bear, all they paid me was just the hundred dollars a day. As time went along, the prices went up gradually until it was five thousand to get a bear. Most of the time, you're dealing with people that got a hell of a lot more money than you have.

All the years Forbes spent chasing bears for his clients taught him a lot about bear behavior and biology.

A bear's size depends on food supply. If he gets lots to eat, he's a big bear. If he doesn't get much to eat, he only grows so big. Admiralty, Baranof, and Chichagof Islands form a group that's in a rain belt. As a result of all the rain, there's lots of streams. There's lots of salmon to run up these streams, so there's lots of food for bears. That's where our big bears are. So that's the three islands we hunted the most. If we wanted to get black bear, we had to go down towards the south end of Peril Straits. There's no black bear where there's brown bear, 'cause the brown bear will kill 'em and eat 'em.

I saw bears digging clams and I still don't know just what they did to get the meat out of the clam. And they'll catch crab and eat them. They're pretty wise as to what the beach has to offer for food.

When there's an ample food supply, the sows will have four cubs. If it isn't quite so good, maybe they'll only have two, or maybe only one. It depends a lot on the food supply. Where there's plenty of salmon, they very often have four. At first I thought they was stealing another bear's cubs, but I realized after awhile that wasn't so. And then the Game Department kinda verified my findings.

When bears walk down a trail, they'll step in the same footprints as the previous bear. You'll find places where it looks just like stepping stones. If you go climbing around on the mountains around here, you'll find bear trails up and over the tops of the mountains, and they all walk in the same footprints, just like stairs. That makes 'em pretty easy to follow.

As time went on, the Forest Service permitted logging at the heads of some of these bays. When a logging outfit moves in, that's goodbye bears. 'Cause the loggers all had to kill a brown bear.

There are other impacts on the bear populations. A male bear will kill cubs and eat 'em. Every time you knock off a big old male bear, that means two to six cubs that's gonna grow up. You're increasing the numbers of bears in the population, but you don't end up with as many big bears. It takes a bear close to 20 years to reach his maximum size. So there might be more bears today, but smaller ones.

Ben's guiding career was very rewarding, but all good things must come to an end. In Ben's case, it was an honorable decision by an honest man.

All in all, it was a very enjoyable career. I was kinda broken-hearted when I had to quit. I lost my left eye and my right eye deteriorated a little bit. I was getting along in years, up in my 90s, and I think there comes a time when you gotta cut it out.

As it happened, I had booked some hunters to come up in '98. I analyzed my own condition and said, "Would I hire a guide like that to take me out bear hunting, when it might be the only time I ever get to do it?" And the answer was "no," so I quit. You gotta live with yourself. I just turned the hunters over to my assistant and let him take them.

I was a bear guide for 50 years. I miss it very much. Here's another funny thing. The year I retired from hunting, we began to see bears around Sitka. I've got an explanation for that. I think that the word got around in the bear community: "Ben's retired, so it's safe now."

{BEN FORBES PASSED AWAY IN 2006, JUST AFTER HIS 100TH BIRTHDAY}

Northern Southeast

Area of detail

Yakutat, Hoonah

KEN FANNING
Yakutat, AK

Ken Fanning was a "military brat," moving repeatedly around the country. Ken's dad was an avid outdoorsman and fostered the same interest in his son. Ken got his first guide and outfitting job in Colorado right after high school. When he came to Alaska for field experience, he knew he'd finally found "home."

I started college at Colorado State in Fisheries and Wildlife Management. To get a degree, you had to have six months of related field work. I got a job with the Alaska Department of Fish & Game. I was headed for the Kvichak River to work on a sockeye weir.

I didn't have any money so I hitchhiked from Colorado to Seattle. I knew there were boats headed to Alaska, so I walked the wharfs looking for a ride. One boat owner agreed to take me as far as Petersburg, if I'd help him paint his boat. Our cargo was 504 cases of beer for the Harbor Bar in Petersburg. A few bottles were lost to 'breakage' during the trip. We had ten days of the most incredibly beautiful weather on the Inside Passage.

When we got to Petersburg, the captain said, "There's no sense in you going up to Bristol Bay when Fish & Game needs help here." Within a week, I was on a boat seeing and smelling and feeling and enjoying what Alaska had to offer. It became obvious to me I didn't need to go back to Colorado.

Fanning transferred to the University of Alaska Fairbanks, but was not totally committed to academic life. He wanted to spend more time outdoors, so he started a series of jobs that included work as a commercial fisherman, assistant guide, and a receiving agent for one of the major taxidermists in the world. All these experiences prepared him for his ultimate job as a hunting and fishing guide.

We started a sport fish guiding operation on the Gulkana River and I worked as an assistant for five different big game guides. Of course, I was trapping in the winter, too.

I figured the price they paid for my furs wouldn't be any higher with a degree or without a degree, so I never graduated. By then, I knew the pay at Fish & Game wasn't very good, either. I decided my future was as a guide, so I eventually got my hunting guide's license.

I started as an assistant guide just after the "same-day airborne" law had gone into effect. Prior to that, it was legal to spot game from a plane, then land and shoot it the same day. A lot of the guides who worked under the old system had trouble getting out of that mold.

One of the guides I worked for certainly fit in that category. He was just an unbelievable pilot and felt obligated to get animals for every client. So he used an airplane to help get animals. I had been warned he was a bandit, but I didn't want to do anything illegal. For him, the challenge was NOT just to get the game. To him, the challenge was to violate the law without getting caught. He was very good at that. He out-flew and out-guessed and out-maneuvered every game warden and federal agent that tried to nab him.

He wanted areas where nobody else was hunting. That meant inside national parks. That first experience taught me a lot of valuable lessons about dealing with people and also about parts of the guiding industry I really didn't like.

Fanning was an avid trapper when he arrived in Alaska. The wilderness and exotic animals he found here further fueled that interest. He spent countless hours on the trail and in the skinning shed. He was a founding member of the Alaska Trappers Association, and served as the organization's editor. He also operated a trapping supply business which catered to local clientele.

I enjoyed trapping, but it sure as hell wasn't a way to make a living. On the other hand, it was a good way to make a young wife very mad. I don't regret any of those early memories. They were tough, but they were a wonderful way to see and feel Alaska in a way few people in the world get to do any more.

A few trappers got to know each other through the Tanana Valley Sportsman's Association (TVSA). We felt there was a need for a group dedicated to trapping. We started the Interior Alaska Trappers Association in 1973. I served on the Board of Directors for several years.

Fanning was pulled into the political arena to defend the outdoor activities he and most Alaskan residents loved. He observed the strengths and weaknesses of the political system. After getting pulled in even further, he eventually broke away.

In 1978, Jimmy Carter signed that 'monument' declaration which closed millions of acres to hunting and trapping. We rounded up all the outdoor groups in Alaska and formed the Real Alaska Coalition. Our goal was to slow down the federal takeover of our land. Somebody had to go to Washington, D.C., to fight that battle. That somebody was me.

In March 1979, the Real Alaska Coalition hosted eleven members of congress at the TVSA Clubhouse in Fairbanks. We tried to convince them the traditional Alaskan lifestyle of traplines and log cabins and dog teams really belonged in all these areas they were creating. We took them on dog sled rides and stayed in trappers' cabins. It didn't take a rocket scientist to figure out you need a shelter in the winter. In addition, when you've got snow cover and frozen lakes and rivers, you're not causing any kind of environmental damage.

Unfortunately, we got our butts whupped. The D2 bill locked up parts of Alaska and put areas off-limit to hunting and trapping. That's where I learned the lesson that you don't have much influence on political decisions from the outside. After that experience, I decided to run for office. In 1980, I got elected to the Alaska Legislature. That is what taught me you don't have much influence on politics from the inside, either. I left the political arena after four or five years.

Fanning guided hunters in several areas of Alaska. Many clients wanted to hunt large coastal brown bears. He followed up on a friend's suggestion he investigate the Yakutat area for this purpose. It led to him owning and operating the Yakutat Lodge, in an area known for spectacular fishing and hunting opportunities.

I took one look and concluded it was the most adrenaline-pumping, spine-tingling, thrilling hunting I had ever been involved in. This area is a jungle. Most places you can't see more than ten to 15 feet in the woods. The streams are teeming with fish and they attract bears.

We've developed ways to float streams very quietly, and we get very close to bears. We've been charged 500 or 600 times, but never been chomped. We've had bears in the raft, pushing on your shoulder with their nose. We've been standing on log jams with bears walking five to six inches under our feet. Our average shot is 10 to 15 yards. You're eating, sleeping, drinking, and thinking brown bear all the time. It's an exciting type of hunt and has given me a lot of respect for a bear's intelligence.

Guides spend so much time in the woods it's almost inevitable Fanning would have a few dramatic experiences.

I've got fairly long legs. One time I had a hunter with a short 'wheel base.' When we came to a downed log, I'd step over it but he would have to scoot around the end. He got upset and started thinking I was doing this on purpose. We came to another log. I stepped over and landed right on the back of a brown bear sleeping in the trail. Business picks up when you do that!! If you step on a bear, by God the world just comes unglued. The bear took off in the direction of the hunter. So not only am I wearing this guy out, I'm also 'flushing' bears to chase him. Of course the poor bear was more scared than either of us.

On another hunt, it was raining cats and dogs, like it frequently does down here. We were sitting on a ledge part-way up a chute where there had been a landslide. The weather was so bad I sent the hunters back to camp. Eventually, I decided to head back to camp, too. I started walking up the hill and the mountain decides it's time for another landslide. Now, I'm headed down a chute towards this raging river with mud up to my knees. The slide lost its momentum and I stopped about eight feet from the edge of the river. I was buried chest deep. My arms were free, so I just started digging out. I finally wiggled out of my backpack, got some tools and dug myself free. When I got back to camp, I looked like I had been through a train wreck.

The passage of the Alaska Lands Act put Fanning and other hunters and trappers at odds with the U.S. Forest Service. As he sees it, their job has become to keep Alaskans from enjoying the Alaskan wilderness.

Their rules and regulations are not relevant to conservation or stewardship of resources. It's more a matter of flexing bureaucratic muscle. That's a negative thing. We ought to kick them out of Alaska. A few years ago, Don Young submitted a bill that would have moved the Alaska headquarters for the Forest Service down to Portland. He asked my opinion. I told him I thought it was a lousy bill.

He said, "I thought you would be in favor of moving them to Portland."

I said, "That's not far enough away. Russia is too close."

Fanning is like most hunters and trappers in Alaska, i.e., he has a strong commitment to doing things the "right way." In this concluding segment, he talks about ethics and his love for the State he now calls home.

One of the great things about hunting and fishing and trapping, particularly in Alaska, is that you are frequently in areas that are beyond the reach of the law. There's a moral judgment to be made between you and the animal and God. If you want to violate the law in a place where you know nobody is watching, you certainly have that option. You have the unique opportunity to develop a moral responsibility. I'd always held to a pretty strict moral code. I believe in fish and wildlife management and I always respected the critters we were pursuing. I always believed in fair-chase hunting.

Alaska has been really, really good to me. I'm glad I got here when I did, and wish I had gotten here a little earlier. The wilderness experiences I've had are worth more than anything money can buy. I'm just grateful every day I wake up and see what is around me.

ADAM GREENWALD
Hoonah, AK

Adam Greenwald was born in Hoonah in 1927, one of a family of ten sisters and four brothers. The family raised livestock and grew vegetables, which they sold to fish canneries and mines in the surrounding area.

My dad came from Germany in the late 1800s. He decided Hoonah would be a good place to homestead. This was during the days of the canned salmon industry. He talked to the superintendents of several saltries and canneries in the area. That was before the days of refrigeration, so they had no fresh meat. He made a deal with them to provide groceries.

We had cattle, pigs, and a team of horses. We had 25 acres of potatoes. We also furnished rutabagas, carrots, cabbage, strawberries, rhubarb, and just about anything you could grow here. We had milk cows and churned our own butter. Dad had a boat named the *Mable G* (after my oldest sister). He'd run from cannery to cannery taking orders. He'd come back home, fill the orders, and then take off and make deliveries. During the 1930s, we lived high on the hog. As far as we were concerned, a "depression" was just a hole in the ground.

Dad dug a great big pit with a manure scoop and a team of horses. It was 20 feet wide, 40 feet long and ten feet deep. On winter weekends, he'd pile it full of snow and all us kids put snowshoes on and we'd tamp it down. We kept that up until it was mounded six or seven feet high above the pit. Then he'd cover it with about a foot of moss. That was our refrigeration. Dad dug a stairway down into the ice and carved holes in the side walls. That's where he'd stick his quarters of beef. In late summer, it would be solid ice in there. It might only be half full, but it would still be ice.

I have lots of good memories of our homestead. I still go over there and pick strawberries and reminisce.

When the kids got all their chores done, they'd do a little fishing.

There was a little stream nearby. We'd peel the bark off of a plant and get the worm inside. We'd tie the worms on the end of a piece of beach grass. We'd lay on our stomachs and lower it down into the stream. As soon as it disappeared, you flipped it, and about 90 percent of the time, a brook trout would come out of the water and fall back in again. If you had your timing perfect, you could flip the trout back behind you into the grass. They were only about four or five inches long.

Back in 1933 or '34, a big yacht anchored right offshore from our farm. The owner was George Eastman, from Eastman Kodak Company. He and a group of his friends were fishing all the rivers in the area.

There were six or seven of us kids fishing those little brook trout. Everybody was screaming and laughing and having a big time. This group of older men from Eastman's boat came walking by, heading for the Pasco River. They stopped when they heard us. Pretty soon, they turned and came walking over. They watched us a while and the next thing you know they laid their split bamboo rods down and they were laying there along with us, catching these brook trout. They were screaming and laughing … just having the biggest time.

They built a campfire, cooked and chomped on those little trout.

They gave us their split bamboo rods. That was the first fishing rod I owned in my life. Our family never owned a fishing rod. We used willow and alder branches and tied a string to it. That was our fishing rod. I'll never forget those millionaires laying on the bank with us and fishing with strands of grass.

Adam's father and brothers taught him the basics of hunting, fishing and trapping. Adam was an eager student. His first mink and deer are still vivid memories. He trapped cooperatively with several family members over the years. It gave him a sense of pride to be helping support his tight-knit family.

In the winter-time, the canneries all shut down, so my dad and all my brothers trapped. I sorta grew up with that. I learned how to trap from my older brother, Albert. I followed him along and saw how he trapped and I tried to emulate him. I helped him skin his pelts and learned a lot of tricks.

The first animals I caught were mink and weasels. There were quite a few around the river flats where we lived. They were easy to catch. Money from the sale of those furs went toward buying my school clothes. It made me feel like I was taking care of myself. I was nine or ten years old.

There were some years we had really bad luck trapping, mostly due to weather. It was so stormy you couldn't get out. When you did get out, all your traps were froze down or buried in snow. It would take you hours to dig them out and get them reset. Then by the time you could get back out, they were buried again. We had a few years that were horrendous. Then I had some super years, too. I averaged around 100 marten, 50 mink, and 25 otter the last eight or ten years.

Years ago, I went trapping with two of my brothers-in-law and one of their brothers. We were trapping up at the head of Port Fredrick. In the evenings, we'd sit around, talking over the day's experiences and pelting our animals. I got through skinning a couple of mine. One of the other guys hadn't skinned an animal before. He was sitting there fiddling with a mink. I said, "You're making it look harder than it is. There's nothing to it. Come here and I'll show you." The mink was partly frozen yet. I was a little careless and I cut the stink bag on the mink. We were down in the fo'castle of the boat and all four of us hit the companion-way at the same time. We were clawing at each other trying to get out of there and get some fresh air.

Alaska isn't an easy place to live or work. Anytime you're working outdoors, a change in the weather can lead to a bad situation.

One of the scariest experiences I ever had was trapping up in Port Frederick in the middle of the winter. Most of the trapping around this country was done with a skiff and outboard.

The weather was so bad I couldn't get out in my skiff for a week or ten days. One day, the wind died down and it turned sort of calm and beautiful. I told my wife, "I'm gonna run up and check that trapline." When I arrived, there was still surf washing on the beach. I anchored my skiff and put my pack-sack on my back. That 'line usually took me an hour to check by skiff, but I figured it was gonna to take all day to hike it. When I got back, it was getting late and starting to blow. I thought, "I'd better get going before it gets too rough and I can't make it home." I pulled in the skiff, jumped in and started up the motor.

I got about halfway across Port Frederick and the motor started dying down. I looked back and could see smoke coming out. I took the cover off the motor and could see it sizzling. It was hotter than a firecracker. I slowed the motor down to an idle and then shut it off. I kept turning the flywheel so it wouldn't freeze up. It finally cooled off enough to restart. I made it back to the beach, but the motor was getting pretty hot. By that time, it was getting pretty dusky and the wind was blowing hard.

I jerked the lower unit off the motor. I saw what happened. When I anchored the boat earlier, I tipped my motor up. The water in the water pump froze. When it's that cold, even salt water freezes. When I started the engine, the ice just wiped out my impeller. I knew better, but I just got sloppy.

The water pump was a flat piece that fit into a slot in the driveshaft. I took my trapping hatchet and chopped off a spruce branch. I took my hunting knife and whittled and shaved it down so it just fit in the pump. By that time, it was getting dark AND cold. I put the motor back together and cranked it up. The prettiest stream of water you've ever seen come out of that back end motor, so I took off.

I knew the shoreline very well. I had been there thousands of times.

By the time I got halfway home, there were big swells and the spray was coming clean over the top of the boat. I was having to run half speed and bailing, too. The boat was covered in ice. I stopped several times and took my trapping hatchet to pound the ice off the boat. When I got home, my wife was worried sick. She thought I was dead and gone. That was one of my scary experiences. I was just lucky.

Over the years, Adam sold his furs to many different furbuyers.

When I was a kid, we sold to Sears Roebuck. I also shipped some to Canada. A few times, I split my orders ... sent half of my furs to one and the other half to another. I was trying to identify the best one. I never did find one that was head and shoulders above the others. They were all pretty competitive.

There was one shipment of furs that brought the biggest price. It was mostly mink and marten, with a few otter. The shipment was missent. It was lost for months. They finally found the shipment in Honolulu, Hawaii. The furs were kept in cold storage. When they finally got to the dealer, he said the fur was in excellent shape. The timing must have been just right, because the prices were quite high. The delay worked to my advantage.

One time, a furbuyer was sitting right here in my living room, tossing marten on the floor, sorting 'em by size and color. He took one and set it over on the side. When he got through, he reached over to grab this one marten and said, "Where'd you catch this?" It was someplace in Port Frederick.

I said, "Why do you ask?"

He says, "In all my years of buying fur, this is the closest I've ever seen to a Russian sable."

He showed me the difference. He gave me a good price on it, but it wasn't a lot more than the rest.

Adam grew up hunting. His older brothers taught him how to shoot and handle a rifle.

I remember one of my first deer hunts. I was with my older brother. I stepped on a twig and it made a little noise. He says, "I'll never take you hunting again. You make too much noise. You spook everything away." He did a lot of deer calling. Sometimes the deer come to the call, but they don't come very fast. You have to have patience. We didn't see anything right away so he decided to move on. I saw a deer head sticking up and a big rack of horns on it. I was seven or eight feet behind my brother. I'd go "psst, psst" making a little noise to get his attention. Finally, he turned around. I pointed up the hill and said, "Behind that log. I can see a deer's head." He looked up and saw it, too. He squatted down, took a bead, squeezed off a shot, and it disappeared. We walked up there and it lay right where it had been. Great big buck. I said, "Albert, good thing you took me with ya. You'd never have got that deer if I hadn't seen it." He finally agreed. Being a little kid, something like that makes you pretty proud.

I remember the first deer I shot. I was 11 years old, trolling for coho. I looked in on the beach and there was a nice big deer walking along the water's edge. I pulled my fishing line in as fast as I could and started rowing in toward the deer without making too much noise. We didn't have outboards in them days. I had a little .303 Savage my older brother gave me. I squatted down in the skiff and took a bead on the deer. I shot and missed. The deer stopped and looked at me and I shot again. There was another guy fishing a couple hundred yards from me. All of a sudden, he started shooting. Then, I shot again and the deer dropped. I rowed in as fast as I could. I got in there and was going to start dressing it out when the other guy came rowing in.

He said, "You know, I was shooting at that deer, too."

I said, "Yeah, but I hit it."

He said, "I don't know about that. I think you'd better give me a hind quarter."

I wasn't going to butcher it up and give it to anybody. I was so proud of that thing. I didn't even finish gutting it. I just dragged it over, put it in my skiff, shoved off, and jumped in. I was afraid that guy was going to get a part of my deer, so I was getting out of there.

Where there are deer, there are also bears. Adam had several run-ins with bears as he got older.

One time, my brother-in-law Art and I were sitting on the edge of a meadow. I pulled out a deer call and I blew on it a few times. I saw my brother-in-law make a motion. I looked over at him and he pointed in back of us. I turned around and saw a bear step over a log. It disappeared into some berry brush. He didn't appear again, so I blew the deer call a couple more times to try to see if he would move. About that time, he came out of the brush and ran straight for Art. I aimed right for the base of his neck and I shot. He went down but got right up and charged me. I hit him in the chest that time and he went down again. He started to get up again so I shot him a third time and finished him. I looked at Art. He was shaking like a leaf. I was half-mad at him. I asked him why he didn't shoot and he said he couldn't get his gun up.

There was another time I had a bear come after me. I was packing a deer out. There was an inch of snow on the ground. I could hear something that sounded like a man walking in the snow. I sat down to take a rest. I kept watching in the direction where I could hear the sound coming from. Pretty soon, this bear came out. I whistled and I figured I'd spook him, but he wanted my deer. So I wound up having to shoot that one. He was pretty ornery. I hunted around bear country quite a bit. I knew how they acted. I felt pretty safe and I was a pretty good shot, too.

Adam was appointed to the Fish & Game Board by Governor Bill Eagan, who he describes as "... just a regular guy." Adam's tenure on the Board was full of controversial issues, some of which were resolved in unexpected ways. He enjoyed the opportunity to travel throughout the State and interact with the "good people" of Alaska.

I was the first troller who ever served on the Board of Fish and Game. There were a couple guys on the Board who I thought tended to feather their own nest a little bit, but for the most part we tried to be honest. They were a pretty good group of guys.

It was educational, but I didn't enjoy the politicking. Too many guys tried to buy our services. That sort of irritated me. I felt like I had to sleep at night. It was taking away from the biological reason for adopting or changing a regulation. I didn't go for that.

Now, Adam reflects on his life, one he thinks was well spent. He's been an outdoorsman his entire life, and enjoyed the hunting, fishing and trapping that made Alaska his paradise.

I've led a quite a varied life. I commercial fished a lot, but I always went back to my trapping and hunting in the fall and winter. For me, it was exhilarating. That's what kept me here. I just loved the hunting and fishing and trapping.

I'm getting to the point in my life where I can't enjoy all the things I used to. What bothers me more than anything is looking at the hills around here that are being logged off. I've packed deer off of pretty near every one of 'em. I can think back on many real fun times I've had there. It's a way of life, and it's sad to see it go away.

ALF SKAFLESTAD
Hoonah, AK

Alf Skaflestad was born in Norway in 1908. He came to America in 1928. Like most other men of that era, Alf faced hard times during the Great Depression. What few jobs were available often paid only room and board. Alf managed to scratch out a living based on fishing, logging, hunting, and trapping.

Three of us came up to Alaska on a little boat. We was planning to go fishing. We didn't know too much about fishing. Fish prices were low until the war [World War II]. You had to grab anything just to survive. There was no jobs. Logging was all closed down.

We wound up in the cannery. It helped out a little bit. We were getting about six dollars a month. After the season was over, you had to wash the salt off the anchor cables and put them through a tar vat. Boy, you got really messy from that stuff.

We went into the winter with no jobs. At that time, there was a market for mink and otter. We scratched around and got a few mink and otters and kept the wolves away from the door. Then the market went against natural fur. The imitation fur took over. You couldn't sell natural fur for a while during the 1930s. It was pretty tough for quite a few years.

We lived off the land. We ate lots of clams and crabs; salmon and halibut. We had deer meat. You've got to respect the animals. They have a right to live as well as we have. They give us part of their living. I don't know what would happen here in Southeast if we didn't have the deers and the clams and so forth when the Depression was on. We had to take the bad with the good. Sometime a little too much bad.

One thing we did to survive was hunting eagles for the bounty. Those days, we used to get two dollars. My brother-in-law Albert was a good shot. He would go to the back of the boat and I would sit out in the front and make motions to distract the eagles. Then, he would shoot from the back. But they got pretty wise. When they see the skiff coming, they took off up the mountain.

Almost all of the skiffs were made locally. Nice row boats. You could easy make five, six, seven miles an hour. If you rowed all the way to the end of the bay, that's 15 miles. We would go one day from here up to the end, and come back the next day. You're trapping and shootin' eagles. Sometimes you come back the same day if there was no game. Later on, we got small gas boats, with a little cabin and a stove. Bad weather, we got to sit inside.

When it got real cold weather, you needed good wool pants. They kept you warm. And rain gear that doesn't leak. We had regular leather boots or waterproof rubber boots. American made in those days. The United States had the finest materials and well-tailored.

Trapping was an important part of Alf's income and lifestyle. He trapped mink and otter to get crucial cash income for his family. Marten were not indigenous to Chichagof Island, where Hoonah is located. They were transplanted after Alf arrived. Introduction of this new furbearer had unintended consequences.

We trapped mostly mink at that time. There was more market for mink. Some years they were up to around $50 to $60 a pelt. I'd get maybe 30 or 35 mink per year. I wasn't a very good trapper. Some people do a lot better than that. Once in a while we'd get otters, too. Otters are pretty smart and a strong animal. They are hard to trap and a lot more work in fleshing.

Marten were transplanted here by the Forest Service. They got pretty thick. Some trappers made a few dollars. I guess they got a pretty fair price for them. The marten is very destructive to a lot of birds. They eat the ptarmigans and grouse. You can hardly hear a grouse hooting any more. I don't know what's the reason for planting them here. Why spend money on something like that?

There was a furbuyer who came through every year. His name was Henry Moses. He liked to get the furs as cheap as possible. He'd find a lot of problem with your furs when he looked them over. That will cut the price. If you didn't like the price he offered, then you could ship them out to one of the auction houses. The problem there is you didn't know how much money you were gonna get. Sears and Roebuck also bought fur in those days.

Logging sustained Alf and his family for many years. He took pride in the hard work.

I worked in the woods for a logging outfit for a couple winters. We did it just to survive. Really no wages to speak of. We had a place to sleep, anyway. The canneries started contracting for pilings and other materials. They would give the contracts to local people for the winters. That's how I got into logging. I would have a small contract for 300 to 400 hemlock trap pilings. I had to do that in the winter 'cause they needed the pilings early in the spring for the traps. When my sons got big enough, I gave them a little experience on the logging operation. They helped a lot.

When I'd go out to the logging area, I'd see bear tracks. It looked like the bear was inspecting to see what was going on. I never had any problems with the bears. We run into quite a few bears but we always had something to protect ourselves and we tried to avoid them. We was always looking out for danger. They are big unpredictable animals.

Of course you had to get firewood for home so you wouldn't freeze to death. We could get the wood during our logging, but it had to be worked up. A lot different in the winter-time when you get four or five feet of snow and it makes different work out of it. You've got to shovel the road so you can get the stuff to your house. The snow piles up pretty high when you shovel everyday for a couple, three months.

Alf enjoyed hunting deer. The venison fed his family. Some winters, he returned the favor.

My favorite place to hunt deer was at the head of the bay. It's facing the sun more on both sides. And the deers survive a lot better there, in a shady place. We had some real bad winters when everything would freeze up along the beach line. It would build up ice from swells. Some years, we had up to 5 feet of snow. A lot of places, you couldn't get off the beach because the snow and ice were built up so bad. Those conditions destroyed a lot of deer some winters. We used to go out and cut down old hemlock right on the beach line. They have long grey moss the deer could eat. There were no dead deers around there. They survived good on that. I used to look forward to go out and help the deer.

Fishing (both sport and commercial) played a major role in Alf's life. It provided meat for the table and cash to pay the bills.

There was lots of halibut. Any place you go, you could get a halibut, except for a certain time in the winter. I think they ran out to deep water. You could pretty near always get a salmon to eat, one or two fish. That's all you need anyways. The fishing was a lot better back then than it is now.

We used to take the family in the big boat and go down to Spasski to sport fish for king salmon. One time, a big halibut came. I had to go in the skiff and follow the halibut a couple miles. It went deeper and deeper and deeper. Eventually, he kinda slacked off. I got him in close and I could club him. That took a lot of clubbing. We couldn't weigh him, but I estimate him around 250 pounds. That was a dandy fish!

We never had an option to negotiate price on fish. The cold storage set the price. That's what you have to sell it for. Our wild fish are a big resource to America, but we are selling it about as cheap as they did in 1930. We need jobs to survive and have a good life here.

Alf has seen his town grow and change in many ways. He still loves it as much as he did when he first arrived. Life in Southeast Alaska is better than anywhere else, in Alf's view.

Hoonah has come a long ways. We didn't even have running water when I first came here. All outhouses. The government has helped quite a bit. When we got our water and sanitation system, that was the biggest improvement. Harry Douglas was the mayor. He made the contacts to incorporate the town. That way you can get a little federal money, and that's how you start progressing.

I think Southeast Alaska is one of the best places to live. There's a lot of food on the beach and in the woods for hard times like we used to have years ago. It was up to you to go and get it.

{ALF SKAFLESTAD PASSED AWAY IN 2007}

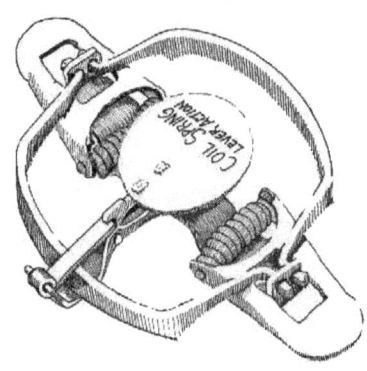

South-Central

Area of detail

Anchorage, Cordova, Sutton, Palmer

RED BEEMAN
Anchorage, AK

Like many sourdoughs, Red Beeman can thank his Uncle Sam for bringing him to Alaska as a soldier. Red fell in love with The Great Land and never left. He took right to the trapping lifestyle.

I trapped the first winter on Eagle River. A couple years later, I had a guy fly me in to the Talkeetna Mountains. When he landed me on that muskeg, he was on wheels and it was frozen. I started packing my camp up to where I was going to set it up. I looked up in a spruce tree and 15 foot up was a Yukon stove tied to a branch. I said, "The snow must get deep in here." Sure enough it got deep. I had to wait for snow to settle before I could start moving. I had a little seven foot by seven foot wall tent and just the top of it was sticking out by the time he could get back in there and get me out.

I got married in 1959. The family and I went to Farewell in '73. The wife taught the kids ... state correspondence school. I had two real good winters there.

I eventually moved to Big River out of McGrath and been there ever since. I've got a good marten 'line over there. My son and I trap it for a year, let it rest for a couple of years and go back in there. I've got my main cabin. I set a tent up on a frame out on the 'line and stay out overnight. One tent and then some loop trails.

I used to like to trap beaver. I'd get my houses marked in the fall so I knew where the feed beds were and where the water was deep. In the spring, I would take some logs and set me up a little lean-to. I would bring those beaver in and skin them there and pack them back to the main cabin. It was a nice time of the year. The days were getting longer and the weather was warmer. I didn't make much money. The hides were selling for $20 or $30. I always figured when they went up to $2,000 per hide, I'd try beaver trapping again.

One of the things I've always enjoyed is getting the trapline ready. Getting your camps ready and getting your traps set up. If you're on the same 'line year after year, you've got all your marten traps hanging and it is just a matter of cleaning things up and prospecting for new fur sign.

I've been on some good traplines and some bad ones. I consider the bad ones to be where the snow was too damn deep.

Red's trapping success can be attributed to his hard work. Red also credits the guys who came before him, taught him what they knew, and helped him when he needed it. There's nothing like experience.

One of them was Oscar Vogel. The first winter he came here was in the late 1920s. He trapped up around Lake Louise, but he didn't really like it. Then he went down to the Alaska Peninsula, but he didn't like that either. He said it was too windy.

Oscar heard of a trapline on the Talkeetna River. He and the owner (a guy named Joe) took their dogs up the Chickaloon River and crossed over onto the head of the Talkeetna River. Joe had four cabins there. As they were working their way from cabin to cabin, they'd occasionally see a big grizzly on the mountain side. Joe would shoot it and just leave it lay.

Oscar asked, "What are you doing?"

Joe said, "Good fox bait."

That's the way it was in those days.

Oscar bought Joe's trapline. He built a cabin at the outlet of Stephan Lake in 1933. The whole time he was working on it, there was a big grizzly getting red salmon out of the creek. Oscar would go about his business and the grizzly went about his business. They didn't work more than 30 yards apart the whole time and never bothered each other.

Oscar's country was mainly marten, wolf, wolverine, and fox. He was well known as a good wolf trapper. He'd take his dog team in there and stay the whole winter. At the end of the season, he would run his dog team down the Chickaloon and into Anchorage.

When Oscar came into Anchorage, he'd stay at the Lane Hotel. He'd give his room number to the furbuyers. He said there were a couple seasons when they never even quibbled over price. They just asked, "How much you gotta have for the furs?" He'd tell them and they'd pay. He was selling silver fox for $700 to $800. At that time, that was what a laborer would make for a whole year's wage on the Alaska Railroad. I'm sure there were some other years when it wasn't so good. Oscar was still trapping there when I guided for him in the 1960s.

########

Another old trapper I knew quite well is a fellow by the name of Roland Osborne. I guided with him, too. When he was 12 years old, his dad told him, "I hate to do it but I have to take you out of school. I bought a trapline up at Montana Creek. You have to go up there and run it."

Ozzie became quite a trapper. He was well known as a snare man. He'd walk up the Matanuska River from Palmer and trap up above Chickaloon. He'd get over 100 coyotes in a season, and at the time they were paying a $30 bounty on them. That was pretty good money in those days.

########

Just before World War II broke out, a trapper had a pilot fly him over near Farewell to trap. The pilot was supposed to come back and get him in January, but never showed up. The war broke out and the feds [had] grounded all the airplanes. The trapper didn't have a radio, so he didn't know what was going on. It was March before the authorities would let the pilot fly again. When the pilot flew back over there to pick him up, the trapper was standing under a spruce tree smoking a cigarette. The trapper said, "Where the hell have you been?"

Red closes with some wisdom of his own.

By nature, I'm a loner. I like being out on the 'line by myself, but that's not always possible in Alaska today. It's hard to find a place by yourself. Of course, there are many areas where there aren't a lot of people, but in those areas there usually isn't much fur, either.

# # # # # # # #

I read an article in which a young trapper asked an old trapper, "How do you catch fur?"

The old guy said, "Remove all suspicion and lay a great temptation."

That's so true. I cut that out of the paper, tacked it up on the wall in my cabin.

# # # # # # # #

That sums up what I've done. Fish in the summer, guide in the fall, trap in the winter. It has been a good life. When I get too old and I can't move anymore, I'm going to miss trapping.

LARRY KRITCHEN
Cordova, AK

Larry Kritchen was born in California, a far cry from Alaska. He was raised on a small ranch in the desert, which gave him ample opportunities to get involved in outdoor activities.

My grandfather was quite a fisherman, so he would take me fishing a lot. My dad was a hunter. He liked to hunt deer no matter what time of year it was. We always had a buck hanging up when I lived on that ranch.

I got my first deer on that ranch when I was 11. We didn't bother the coyotes until they started killing our turkeys. Then we started trapping.

Like many people who move to Alaska, Larry came for the adventure and stayed because of the lifestyle and myriad opportunities it offered.

In '49, my wife's stepdad had a salvage and freight business here in Cordova. I always wanted to come to Alaska. I had a job waiting with him, so I came up.

Cordova was smaller back in the 1950s. People were real friendly and you knew everybody in town. There wasn't any TV and the biggest businesses in town were the saloons. They had a brothel down the street. There was wide-open gambling ... six card rooms and a few slot machines. It was a "Wild West" town. When I came up here, I couldn't believe it.

We freighted up and down the coast. We had a big landing craft and we hauled oil in drums and unloaded it by hand. We also did some logging on Montague Island. I was only going to work for a year and then go back, but I decided to stay.

I bought a hunting license for ten bucks, and a fishing license for ten bucks. You could seine, gillnet, dig clams, fish halibut, hunt deer, so I did all that stuff.

There was a bounty on eagles and seals at that time. Seals were six bucks a piece and the bounty on eagles was two dollars. Standard wages were $1.75 an hour. I was a pretty good rifle shot, so I could make some pretty good money.

The seal hides were really beautiful. I thought it was a crime to just claim the bounty and throw away the hide, so I started salvaging some of the hides. I talked some of the Natives into selling me their hides so I started in the fur business with seals. I've had a fur buying license since 1950.

Living in Cordova, it was inevitable Larry got involved in commercial fishing. The money was good, but came with inherent hazards.

First time I ever went commercial salmon fishing, a friend of mine loaned me his gear. Red salmon were selling for $1.25 apiece. The first set I ever made, I got 64 reds in an hour. I was getting paid 35 bucks a week working for the City. After that, I went fishing.

The first year I fished, I rented a boat from the cannery for 50 bucks.

The canneries gave you free bread, free meat and when you delivered fish, they usually give you a six pack of beer. In the winter-time, they'd buy all your groceries and put them on your bill. Everybody was on credit.

I also fished halibut out here in the bay. For big fish, we got five cents a pound. For mediums we maybe got 14 cents. When the big halibut schooners came in, they'd sell their old gear for five bucks a skate, so we didn't have much for expenses. The biggest halibut I caught was 250 pounds.

I had halibut hooks in my hands a couple of times. One time I was laying out gear with the tide and it was whistling out pretty fast. One of the hooks grabbed my knuckle. I had to hold onto to the roller until it ripped out. The doctor's office used to have a bunch of hooks hanging up that he took out of halibut fishermen.

Trapping has been a nearly life-long love for Larry. Fortunately, he found a trapping partner who shared that passion.

In the wintertime, everybody trapped. I wanted to trap, too. In '49, I bought a non-resident license. I didn't know anything about trapping mink. One day, I caught what must have been the dumbest mink in Prince William Sound. That was my first fur, and trapping was real interesting.

I heard Jim Webber trapped more fur than anybody else in the area around Cordova. I ran into Jimmy trapping down the river. He had something like 20 mink. We got talking and he said, "We'll go partners and trap around here." Jimmy taught me everything I knew about trapping. Jimmy and I trapped together for many years. The first ten years we probably made more money trapping than we did fishing.

We had 100 miles of snowshoe trail. We were in good shape. We'd go goat hunting and we'd run back down with the meat. Now I can't hardly walk down the hill.

Mink were one of the mainstays for trappers on the Copper River delta.

We'd probably average 30 bucks for mink. Wages were only 35 dollars a week. If we caught ten mink in a day, that was big money. We were trapping right out of town. We didn't want anybody to know about it, so we kept our mouths shut. We'd average between 40 and 100 mink every year.

The worst mink season we ever had we only got 19 mink. The reason was it just snowed and snowed and froze and there was no way you could keep traps working. I even had trouble getting around.

When there were huge tides, it would flood most of the Delta. The mink would all head towards the timber where we had traps along the road. We used to trap up and down the creeks and walk hundreds of miles for mink. After we wised up, we just set one trap on each side of that creek and we got every mink during the season. We didn't have to go hunting for them. They hunted for us.

Beaver also brought in a steady source of income for Larry and Jimmy.

We also trapped beaver. The limit was only ten when we first started. We always got our limits. Then beaver prices started to drop and a lot of people didn't like to go through chopping ice like we did. Sometimes we would go through five feet of ice for beaver. They kept raising the limit up until it got to 40.

We never got a big price on beaver. I think the best we ever did was 40 bucks average, but money was different. A week's wages was 35 bucks and a beaver is worth 35 bucks. I'd rather catch one beaver than work all week.

I did pritt' near all the skinning of our beaver. I could do a blanket-sized beaver in five, six minutes. The secret is the knife. I don't know how to describe the method. I can't explain it. I just do it.

Lynx were rare, but a fun diversion from the normal spectrum of species available near Cordova.

When we first started trapping, nobody had caught lynx around here for years. One year, we caught a couple and then they came by the millions. Unfortunately, they were only worth about ten bucks. They come down here looking for rabbits. As soon as the rabbits are gone, then the lynx vanish again.

Wolverines were relatively abundant in the area. Live-trapping them led to some interesting experiences.

We caught a lot of wolverines. At one point, we had four live wolverines here in cages. We were using leg-hold traps with padded jaws. One of those wolverines was so tame I could reach in and scratch his ears and he would eat beaver meat out of my hand and then lick my hand.

We sold two live wolverines to Walt Disney for the movie "White Wilderness." We received 700 bucks. We didn't know what we were dealing with or we would have got more money.

Trappers on the Delta grew accustomed to an abundant muskrat population.

There used to be quite a few muskrats here. One winter we got bored. We were waiting for beaver season to open so we trapped 'rats from a pond 10 miles out of town. We had twenty traps, and we caught 70 'rats the first day. We caught 500 'rats out of that pond in two weeks and then quit.

As in many Alaska communities, hunting was a major activity for most of the men in Cordova. They valued the red meat as a supplement to the fish they caught. Larry was no exception. The pursuit of mountain goats presented many challenges.

Jimmy and I killed lots of deer and goats. We were tough. The places we went would now take me six months to get back there. We'd take these old Army parkas and a piece of Visqueen and that was about it. We did have an old coffee pot to make hot water. Sometimes we'd be gone a couple three days. I'd tell my wife, "If we don't come back in a week, you can look for us. Other than that, don't worry."

One time we were back there about ten miles. We snuck up on these goats on a ridge. We passed up a great big old monster. We didn't want no part of him. But there was about six yearlings laying down. Jimmy said, "I'll take the one on the right and you take the one on the far left. When I shoot, you shoot." He never misses, but he missed that time. I never got a shot.

The goats ran and jumped off a cliff. I ran and looked over the edge. I see a goat down there about 30 yards. After that, it is 1,500 feet straight down to the bottom. This is happening really quick so I just shot him and he goes all the way down 1,500 feet. We had to go clean around and down below on this slide to get to him. It wasn't one of the yearlings. The thing was as big as a full grown Shetland pony. It must have weighed 400 pounds. Jimmy was mad at me for killing that monster.

We got it all cleaned up and we hung the hide for a windbreak. We built a big fire and had a really neat place for a camp. It was really cold and in the middle of the night it started snowing.

That night, Webber was cold so he kept snuggling up closer to the fire. I woke up once and smelled something peculiar burning. I soon realized Jimmy was on fire. I started throwing snow on him and he got mad at me.

He said, "What are you doing?"

I said, "You're on fire and I'm putting you out."

That next morning, we had two-and-a-half feet of snow. We thought it was going to be a job getting out of there. We went about a mile and there was no more snow. Then we were home free.

Goat meat can be tough, but we were not going to waste it. We tried everything to cook that goat. Finally, we gave it to the children's home and they raved about it. They ground it all up and put it in chili.

One year, Jimmy needed some meat, so we went over to the mountain. We found a big billy and about ten feet away was nice little kid. Jimmy shoots the kid. The bullet ricochets and hit the big old billy, so he had to kill him. We ate half of that kid in one sitting. So Jimmy has this big old goat hanging up outside the cabin. He put the loins in a pressure cooker and put meat tenderizer on it. He said every day the meat was the same ... just like a baseball. A week later, a wolverine came by and took down the carcass, but left it. He didn't want it either.

They also spent many days afield hunting for deer.

One time, I was fishing silvers on the flats with another guy. We each had our own boat. It was pretty early in the season and there weren't any fish. I says, "Heck with it. Let's go deer hunting." So we go over to Hawkins Island. The next morning we went way up on top of this mountain. I saw this buck and he took out of there like a shot. It was the biggest deer I had ever seen in my life. He got away because I had my gun on my shoulder and wasn't alert. I went back down and I told my hunting partner, "I'm going back there tomorrow and get him."

The next morning, the deer wasn't exactly where I thought he would be. I went up on another ridge and saw him sneaking away. WHAM!! I got him. I put my sling around his horns and tried to drag him, but I couldn't. I could carry a 150-pound buck on my back at the time, but I couldn't even drag this deer. I cut him in two and I packed half of him out. My partner shot a deer that weighed probably 130 pounds. The front half of my deer weighed way more than his whole deer.

Ptarmigan hunting gave Larry and Jimmy a chance to help out the local senior citizens.

I love to hunt ptarmigan. One time back in the '50s, there was a flock of ptarmigan out here that must have been 5,000 birds. The old timers around here liked to eat ptarmigan. They couldn't hunt anymore, so Jimmy and I would go hunting and fill backpacks with ptarmigan. We'd bring them back to town for the old timers.

Like most Alaskan hunters, Larry has a few bear stories to share.

I had a colonel in the Army hunting with me one year. We crossed this river in the morning when the water level was down. That afternoon we tried to get back to camp and the river was up. It was getting dark so we were going up and down the other side of the river trying to figure out how to get across. All of a sudden I heard something. About 40 yards across the river was a sow running around in circles clicking her teeth and roaring. She had three cubs. They were two year olds. I told this guy, "Don't move. Be quiet. Don't do nothing."

The wind was going right to her. Nobody had hunted in that country for years, but she was mad at us for being there. All of a sudden, she jumped in the water and come swimming across. When she got halfway across I yelled, "Get out of here bear!"

On our side it was all timber. I hear her coming through the brush, clicking her teeth and roaring. I couldn't see her until she was ten feet away. I had an ought-six with 180 grain bullets and I shot her point blank in the chest. She just turned to the side and went into the brush. The cubs went right with her. I went and looked. There was blood everywhere. I said, "She's dead, but we're not going in there tonight." We finally got across the river. Early the next morning, we went back over there. She was deader than a mackerel.

You take a hunter who can hit a dime at 100 yards and when they shoot at a bear with a dead rest, they'll miss. It will take off running and you've got to shoot him before he gets in the brush. I had to do that several times. The guys just get nervous.

I'll tell you how nervous one guy got. We were waiting on a trail for a bear to come by. Finally, here comes this bear. He turned broadside at about 125 yards. I said, "Shoot him right through both front shoulders." The hunter had a .338 Weatherby with a dead rest and we knew the distance. He shoots and breaks the bear's front foot. I see him taking off for the brush, so I dumped him. The hunter keeps shooting. I said, "The bear is dead." I figured there were going to be a lot of bullet holes because he shot five times. I skin it out. There was only one bullet hole and it was mine.

We get back to camp and this guy tells his partner what a great gun this .338 is. I'm wondering if I'm hallucinating or the hunter is. The next day, his partner and I go to the same area to hunt. I picked up all that spent brass and threw it in the river so he wouldn't see it.

Another guy hit a bear in the foot with a .300 Weatherby. We had this bear cold turkey. The bear was fishing, so he wasn't paying attention to other things. The wind was in our favor. I said, "We can sneak right up on this bear." We got 100 yards away. He'd go out and catch a silver, bring it up, eat one bite, and go get another one.

I says, "As soon as he comes up with another fish, I'll tell you when to shoot." The bear came up with a fish and turned broadside. I says, "Shoot him right through both shoulders." He shoots and breaks the bear's front foot. The bear takes off running and I had to shoot him. I look at the guy. He's holding his gun in one hand and the bolt in the other hand. He says, "That's the second time this rifle has done that." I said, "Why did you bring it?"

Larry respected the local game wardens, but that didn't mean all of their interactions were cordial. Larry wasn't above playing a few tricks on the officers.

Fred Robard was a warden back in Territory days. Jimmy and I were hunting eagles for bounty. We go out to Power Creek, which was a game reserve. There was a lot of eagles out there. It was closed for any kind of hunting, but we didn't know it. We had the glove compartment door down and had about four sets of eagle claws sitting there. That is what you kept for the bounty. We went out in the woods and up the creek and through the brush. We came back and the U.S. Fish & Wildlife truck is right behind us.

Fred's partner says, "This is a game reserve. You can't hunt in here. It's illegal. If we ever catch you hunting eagles in here again you've had it." A real nice guy. We never did that again.

########

We made Fred mad one time. We caught a big muskrat. Beaver season wasn't open. We stretched that 'rat round, like you would with a beaver. We told Fred we got a beaver by accident and asked if he could tag it. He came out and God he got mad. He didn't take the joke too well.

########

That isn't even the best one. An enforcement agent trapped us once. We were out scouting the day before the season opened. We came out from under a bridge and here's the Fish & Wildlife going by with their truck and they saw us. When the season opened the next day, those guys kept following us out the road. Every time we'd get out of our truck to look at a trap they'd get out and follow us.

One day, we had a mink and they said, "You're under arrest."

I said, "What for?"

"Trapping out of season."

I said, "The season has been open for a week."

They said, "This trap was set before the season."

I said, "It wasn't set before the season. We just put it there."

They said, "If you guys go along with this, we'll charge one of you $25."

I wasn't going to do it because we were framed.

Jimmy finally said, "I'll pay the damn fine."

Three days later those guys came up and asked us to skin a sea otter.

I skinned it and says, "That'll be 50 bucks." That was my way of getting even.

The guy went berserk. He said, "We don't have that kind of money."

I said, "Well, that's the price."

He said, "I'll tell you what we'll do. When you get gas down at Hoover's, you tell them it is for 'Activity 97'."

We agreed to that. So, every time Jimmy and I got gas to go trapping, put it on "Activity 97." Free gas for the rest of the season.

#########

There was another enforcement officer by the name of Mills. He was pretty nice guy after I got to know him. I was trapping coyotes. I found a dead moose. Somebody apparently shot it during the hunting season and lost it. It was about two miles off the road. There were lots of coyote tracks, so I made about five snare sets. They weren't near the moose but within 300 yards of it. One day, I go down there and sure enough I had one coyote. Here comes Mills.

He says, "I'm going to arrest you for using the moose for bait."

I said, "My traps are 300 yards away from this moose."

He was planning to arrest me, but I finally talked him out of that. Later on we got to be really good friends.

Larry could have chosen any town in Alaska to live. Looking back, he's glad he made Cordova home.

Our outdoor lifestyle here in Cordova has meant everything to us. All my kids were raised on deer and goat meat. They all still hunt. Within the family, we kill lots and lots of geese and ducks. My one boy still traps.

We pick a lot of berries. I've got five gallons of salmonberry wine going right now. Then we pick mushrooms and we smoke fish. We've been lucky. There is no other place like Alaska as far as I am concerned. It's been a good life.

{LARRY KRITCHEN PASSED AWAY IN 2010}

JUNE MOORE
Sutton, AK

June Moore was raised on a Depression-era farm in Iowa. She came to Alaska with a military man who was stationed at one of the posts.

My father was an auctioneer. He traveled and I had to practically run the farm. So I grew up knowing what hard work was. I wrestled those cows and horses around.

My father was a great hunter and fisherman. He was the person that kind of motivated me. My dad trapped and I used to toddle along behind him and have trouble getting through the fences. He said, "If you can't keep up, stay home." I grew up to be a pretty tough outdoor girl.

I moved to Seattle and I worked in a dental office. My husband was in the service when we met. He came home one day and said, "You better pack your clothes. I have been transferred to Alaska." I said, "Where in the hell is Alaska?" We later separated.

Within a few years of arriving in Alaska, June bought Mentasta Lodge on the Tok Cut-Off. It became the focal point for many of her hunting adventures.

We made a lot of money in the lodge while we were there. We were just nine miles from Mentasta Village where the Natives live. I'm good friends with all of them. We ran the Lodge for 12 years. I hunted out of there. Hunting season was my big relief from the Lodge. When we sold it, I was really happy.

My husband used to take a dozer over and fix a skating rink for the kids. The village all liked us. They all say they wish we were back again. Not me. I got tired of that. Running a lodge is a tiresome thing. Work, work, work.

########

We had a runway adjacent to the Lodge. Kids were playing out there one Sunday. One little kid run in and said, "There's a bear out there." I grabbed my rifle and went out. Sure enough, there was a black bear circling the building. I thought, "I've got to keep an eye on him." He got too close, so I nailed him. I was afraid he would catch one of them kids.

########

I was tending bar at the Lodge one Sunday. I had an old pack horse out in the barn, maybe 500 yards from the bar. A damn bear got in there and killed that horse while we are all sitting at the bar. He drug it out of the corral and up a trail.

I asked a friend, "Will you tend bar? I'm going to go get that bear. If I don't, he'll be back for another one." Another friend by the name of Herb asked to go along.

I said, "OK, but you gotta keep your mouth shut. You can't say a word."

We went up the trail and I knew what I was going to find. The horse is laying there and that bear is raking it from the head all the way back to the hind end. Old Herb's eyes got about that big!

He whispered in my ear, "I never shot a bear before."

I said, "I haven't either."

I knew damn well Herb wouldn't hit the broad side of a barn, so I said, "Aim for his head."

I shot the same time he did and we got him. Herb dropped everything (even his gun) and run all the way back to the bar.

He hollered to everybody, "I got a bear, I got a bear!!"

I never said anything different. It don't pay to hurt somebody. He was a happy old boy. A few guys went up in the pickup and loaded up the bear and brought him down. They parked in front of the garage. I had a big old nosey tom cat. He jumped up there in the pickup and landed right on top of that bear. When he jumped again, he went about 14 feet straight up and 15 feet this way on a dead run. When he left, every hair stood straight out. He looked like a Halloween cat. He didn't come back for three days.

Bill Ellis was a pilot and a guide who lived on the Nabesna Road. He and June often went hunting together.

Bill got a huge monstrous grizzly one year. He had it mounted standing up. His wife and I are good friends. One time, I was at their house and we put a set of diapers on that bear. Boy, did Bill get mad. We thought it was funny, but it really torqued him off.

Bill passed away of a heart attack last year. It broke my heart. We were friends for 35 years.

Hunting polar bears out of Barrow with Ellis was one of June's greatest adventures.

I guided for polar bear in Point Barrow with Bill. One time, we flew out over the Arctic Ocean in a Super Cub and came across some bear tracks. You've got the big pressure ridges and then it's smooth like a road in between. We saw a bear on the other side of a pressure ridge. Bill flew way down and landed. I walked back and hid behind a pressure ridge. That old bear came over the hump and the first shot I got him right in the rear end. After that, he was running, but the next time I nailed him. Nice bear, ten foot, two inches. I was using a .300 H&H Magnum.

One time, we had two German hunters. Bill landed and caught one ski under a pressure ridge and broke it off. He couldn't fly to hunt any more that way, but he had to get us all back to Barrow. We always used the buddy system; two planes fly together. When one lands on the ice, the other one stays in the air. Our other plane landed. We put the two hunters in the back of the Super Cub, and that's a tight fit. Then, they threw me right on top of their lap just like a sack of oats. We were so overloaded we came in tail first when we landed. Luckily, Bill was a real good pilot. He could fly anything. I'd trust my life with him. I did a lot of times.

Bill landed on the ice one day and had trouble with the engine. Our "buddy" pilot landed and took all of us back in. The weather was bad for 30 days, so Bill couldn't get out to retrieve his airplane. By the time he was able to get out to look for it, it was gone. Other pilots flew over that area every day and they told him his plane had drifted on the solid ice pack 35 miles. Hard to believe, isn't it?

June and Bill also hunted other species in other areas.

We hunted goats near Cordova, too. You fly over a glacier into a small lake. There's only one way in and out by airplane. Goat hunting is hard work. When you got to climb up those mountains just like a goat, you earn it.

All the guys were sound asleep at four o'clock in the morning when it was daylight. I got up and climbed up the hill and looked around and there was a goat. I looked him over pretty close and decided he was a good one. I shot him and the damn thing fell over the cliff. So I went down after him and gutted him out.

Bill finally woke up and saw my predicament. He had a great big rope he dropped down from the plane. I hooked onto the goat and he pulled it up. He flew back to camp and dumped him off. Then, he come back and did the same thing with me. I hung onto that rope and he pulled me up and dropped me on the cliff. I never held onto anything so tight in my life. I didn't want to be carried that way very far.

June made the decision to get a license and become a full-fledged big game guide.

I was one of the first women guides. You have to go before an examining board. There were nine or ten men on it. They throw questions at you for an hour. Then you have to take a written test. It was a tough test. You had to know guns, ammo, wildlife biology, hunting regulations. They didn't miss a thing. These guides all knew me, so I wasn't too worried.

I went to lunch and waited for the results of the test. There were 180 men and I was the only woman who took the test that day. Not one of those suckers would buy me lunch. This one guy came to the doorway and said, "You flunked your test." Then he said, "Nah, you didn't. You passed with flying colors." I felt like getting up and pasting him one.

I actively guided pretty close to 20 years.

Dall sheep hunting is a challenge for any hunter.

We hunted for sheep quite a bit. I'd run over those hills more than the sheep did. You learn when you climb a shale slope that when it starts sliding you can go over a cliff. No way you can get out of it. If possible, you want to stay away from it. If you have to cross it, you don't walk, you run. I never fooled around with shale very much. It is dangerous.

My first sheep, I was all by myself. I walked up a canyon. He was on the cliff and I got him. I thought, "How in the hell am I going to get him out of here?" But I managed. He wasn't a big one, thank heaven. I never got a record book sheep. I was more after meat than trophies.

Where it was appropriate, June preferred to hunt by horseback. It made things easier.

You can ride up on animals without spooking them. For example, a moose will stand there and look at you. You stand a better chance of getting a moose when you're on a four legged animal. Moose don't run like they do from something else.

At one time I had 17 head of horses, but right now I'm down to two. I hunt for myself but I don't guide anymore, so I don't need them.

June's primary hunting camp was in the Mentasta Mountains, not far from her lodge.

We hunted mostly moose and caribou. I had a metal camping trailer half-way back in the Mentasta Mountains. My ex-husband was along one time and we also had a friend from Fairbanks, him and his wife. We had a bear right by the door off and on throughout the night. I had to go to the bathroom so I went around the end of the trailer and dropped my drawers. Pretty soon … WOOF! Goddamn grizzly was right on my butt. I banged on the door and yanked it open.

I said, "There's a grizzly right on my tail."

My husband said, "Oh really." He couldn't care less. There were a lot of things like that to laugh about.

One time, I had two hunters that had been out all day and no luck. The hunters were in the cabin drinking. They were not going out again that day. I stepped out of the cabin and it was almost dark. I would never walk out of that cabin without my gun in my hand. I looked up at the outhouse and I see this old antler turn. I never said anything to the hunters. The moose finally stuck his whole head out and I nailed him. He rolled all the way down the hill right next to the cabin.

I said to the hunters, "Okay get out there and get busy. I did your dirty work." I made them clean him.

Hunting has been half of my life. I've done it for years. My favorite place in the world is my hunting camp near Mentasta. It is a beautiful trip in there by horseback. The scenery is fantastic.

When my husband passed away, he wanted to be cremated and his ashes spread over our hunting camp. I put him across the creek and that earthquake came and it really shook everything up. I figure it threw him right back across the creek on my side again.

A lifetime and career hunting wild animals is rewarding, not just in terms of meat and money, but experience as well. June has dozens of stories about her hunts.

I had one hunter who wanted two grizzlies real bad; one for him and one for his buddy. I took them down to the lake back at my hunting camp and there was two grizzlies laying side by side. They were light colored ... beautiful. I learned a long time ago when you've got a greenhorn hunter he freezes up. So when he shoots ... I shoot. The hunter never knows the difference. He got ready to shoot and I shot the same time. The bullet went through both of them and killed them both. Boy, he thought that was a hell of a shot. I told him what a magnificent thing he had done.

I got along good with all of my hunters, I really did. Most of them were non-residents. I've been very fortunate in hunters. I had a good bunch. I didn't really have any bad ones.

I never went out specifically for caribou. They come through the camp back there in the valley. Once in a while I shot one because they were handy and we needed winter meat, but I never cared for hunting caribou.

One incident really shook my cage. I was riding my Appaloosa and it was cold and the ice was coming down the creeks. I started to cross this little creek and the damn horse slipped and fell right on top of me. I was sopping wet and cold. Luckily, I was only a mile from camp and it didn't take me long to get back there. We had a good fire going.

I've hunted in rain and snow and cold ... you name it. You have to do what you have to do, weather be damned. If you wait for the weather to change, you might just sit there all winter. We've got a big Quonset hut with bunk beds. It's real cozy. If you are going to take hunters out in the cold all day, you want to be warm and comfortable when you get back to camp.

I'm left-handed with a rifle and right-handed with a pistol. I've never been gun-shy. I know a lot of people flinch when they shoot but not me. I use a .300 H&H Magnum to hunt grizzly bears, so that will knock anything down. I don't push a bear. That is what torques them off. You just kind of sit down and wait.

All the agency people knew me and they were very nice. I have never broken a game law. I figure if you're going to hunt, do it right. I don't believe in poaching.

Every guide has to know how to field-butcher the animals taken by their clients. June became adept at the process and remains confident she could still handle a large animal by herself.

I can still butcher a moose by myself. Hell, yes. I'm capable, believe me I am. It don't take me long to gut a moose out. You take a rope and tie one hind leg up to a tree and spread the legs. It is not all that hard. You want to drain him of blood as soon as you can. I just start at the tail and take my knife and go right up the belly and I take the liver, heart and lungs out. I cut the head off. That's a messy job.

Moore has great memories of her life in Alaska.

Alaska has been good to me. I'm 83 years old. I've had a lot of fun. I've lived a hell of a life for a woman. I've done things most women would never get a chance to do. God has been good to me. I am totally grateful.

One last parting comment from this tough woman with a twinkle in her eye and a smirk on her lip, when asked if there's anything else she'd like us to know.

Nothing I dare tell you.

{JUNE MOORE PASSED AWAY IN 2006}

MARLIN GRASSER
Palmer, AK

Marlin Grasser was born in North Dakota. When he had free time as a kid, you could find him hunting or fishing. Little did Marlin know the future course of his life had already been established.

M y dad trapped during the Depression. I followed him around on his trapline. Money was pretty scarce and you did whatever you could to make a dollar.

My uncle came up to Alaska in the 1930s. He had a hardware store in Anchorage. He always told me how good the hunting was up here. I would have come up here sooner, but Mother didn't approve of that. I had to finish high school before she'd let me go. I got out of school one day and the next day I was on a plane coming north and never went home.

Naturally, Marlin started hunting close to home, in the Chugach Mountains of Southcentral Alaska. Then he started guiding other hunters. He built his business slowly, bit by bit, tents to cabins, primitive to relative luxury. But Marlin wasn't the only hunter or guide, and the business can be competitive.

I hunted the Chickaloon River, Boulder Creek, and the Oshetna country for moose, caribou, grizzly, goat, and black bear. When I first went over there, it was good hunting. Nobody had been in there on the ground in years. Airplanes had taken hunters in there previously, but they're limited to how far they can go. With the horses, I was unlimited where I could go. It was kinda my private hunting area in those days. You get kinda spoiled. Overall it was just a good experience.

Back in the 1940s, the federal government poisoned the wolves out of the Talkeetnas. It took four or five years before we noticed the sheep and moose populations starting to come back. The wolves started to increase and I lost 14 head of horses to the wolves. These people that want to protect every wolf, I don't know what the hell they're thinking. We manage and harvest all the other animals, but they don't want you to do a damn thing with wolves.

I started out hauling in tents with the horses. I later began building cabins where I needed 'em. I ended up with four cabins. Most of 'em were 12 feet by 14 feet, with four bunks and a table and a stove in the corner. Tents were nice. They're better than no shelter. But it's hard to beat a nice, warm cabin with a wood fire going in the stove.

There was one old guide who hunted in that Hicks Creek country ever since I was kid. One September, I shot a nice big bull caribou up there. I butchered it and took half out one day. I went in the next day to get the other half. I was coming down the trail with a big pack on my back. I had about another hour to get to the road. I ran into this guide who was taking in some gear with his horses. He wanted to talk. I couldn't set the pack down, because there was no way to get back up. He was sitting on that damn horse, B.S.ing with me. He and I both knew what he was doing. He was trying to wear me out. He probably didn't like to see me hunting in there. I finally told him, "I've had enough of this," and I took off.

Marlin shifted his guiding operation to the Wrangell Mountains, east of Glennallen. The first year, he took pack horses into the area from the Alaska Highway near the US/Canada border. It wasn't always easy. In fact, it could be downright treacherous. Swimming horses across raging rivers is quite a feat, especially for a guy who lacked one important skill.

Hunting over in the Wrangells was just one adventure after another. It's beautiful country, and it's big country. You don't just run up and down them mountains very often.

On that glacier, you just take your time, and don't go doing foolish things. I always carried a walking stick and "sounded" everything to make sure it was safe. I put up rock monuments so I could see the trail I'd made going across, 'cause there were no landmarks. When I came back out at the end of September, you could see where the ice had melted a good foot away from those monuments.

When I started hunting in the Wrangells, we swam horses across the Copper River. Horses are powerful swimmers and you pick the best places to cross. I found one place I thought was pretty good, and we didn't have much trouble crossing there. I can't swim, but I don't think it'd do you much good in that river, anyway.

Marlin once again expanded his guide business, this time to the Alaska Peninsula. His clients shot record book moose, caribou and brown bears. Some of Alaska's wildlife makes you work pretty hard for your meat and/or trophy.

We built a lodge on the Alaska Peninsula, southwest of Mother Goose Lake. It was a real comfortable place. We had four cabins and five boats on the river. We had two 180s and a Super Cub. We had all five species of salmon and arctic char. We flew out for rainbow and grayling. The fishing is so darn good some of the clients would just lay their pole down and rest. The fish just wore 'em out.

One time, I had two hunters and needed a moose for one of 'em. We spotted four big moose from the airstrip. I never carried a gun when we were moose hunting. The hunter was the only one that had a gun. The moose were about 250 yards away. He shot and down the old moose goes. The hunter wanted to get some pictures, so he gave me his gun. I'm in the lead walking over there. We were about 30 feet away, and that old moose jumps up. I'm looking up in those big old bloodshot eyes, and hollered to the hunter, "You getting any pictures?" I turned around and they were both running the other way, as fast as they could go. I turned back and shot from the hip and dropped him. That was an exceptional moose. The rack weighed an honest hundred pounds. One ham weighed a hundred and sixty-eight pounds when he took it to the butcher. Back in the early days down on the Alaska Peninsula, I don't think we ever took a moose under sixty-some inches.

But the humans weren't the only ones doing the hunting – the bears were pretty good at hunting, too. And a wounded bruin is a most dangerous adversary.

We were down on the Alaska Peninsula looking for a big bear for one of our hunters. We were checking an old moose gut pile. No bears had been on it. We always circled those gut piles at a distance. We never went directly in to it. We had two or three inches of snow that night. When we checked the gut pile the next day, we ran into tracks of a big ol' bear. Now we could track him. It took us about two hours to catch up with him. He knew we were following him. He was trying to lose us. He'd go up the hill, down the hill, back-switching, and several other tactics. At one point, we stepped out of some brush. He was up the head of the valley, looking over his shoulder right at us. We were 400 or 500 yards apart. It seemed like he knew right where we were gonna come out.

I had the hunters stand at good observation points. I went in the brush, following his trail. He stopped and was sitting on his butt when I come up out of a deep wash. We were about 30 yards apart. He let out a big woof and charged. I swung and shot from the hip and down he goes. I figured, "That's the end of you." I was going to give him another one and the rifle didn't fire. I got a little excited then. I put another round in … same thing. Third time, I figured it was something wrong with my rifle.

Too late to run then, 'cause he was coming after me. No place to get away in the brush. I put my arm up in front of my face and he just slapped that out of the way. I went over backwards, my left leg flew right up by his head and grabbed it in his mouth. I'm laying on my back, watching him with my leg in his mouth. I figured he was gonna bite my leg off, but he didn't. He bit me six or seven times. He let out a big WOOF and walked over me. I just laid there, didn't move. Finally, I just turned a little bit and could see he went down the trail.

There was blood all over the place. I didn't know if it was mine or his. I could move my foot, so I figured nothing's broke. I looked at my rifle. When I was going through those wet alders, a seed from an alder pod got stuck in the sear. The bolt still slid, but it didn't cock the firing pin. I took the bolt out and slapped it on the stock of the rifle, and that jarred it loose. I checked my rifle and had three shells left.

I went back down and asked the hunter to go get the airplane, so we wouldn't lose the bear. The hunter took off and the plane flew over a few minutes later, just by chance. I got his attention by waving my coat. When he looked down, he could see blood all over the snow. The pilot hollered at me the bear was at the top of the alder patch. I go way around the alder patch and start zig-zagging in. I got 60 or 70 feet away, and he come charging out of there. I shot and he turned. I shot again. I couldn't tell if I hit him or not. I tried to go around that patch to get ahead of him before he could get down to the creek. The creek was real brushy and I didn't want him to get in there. I couldn't do it. My leg was starting to bother me. By the time I got around there, he had already beat me.

I was standing there thinking about it, when he walks out right underneath me, 40 or 50 feet away. I hollered at him again and he started to stand up, but he was just too weak. I took my time and shot him right behind the shoulder. Then I set there and whistled and threw sticks down at him, 'cause all I had was my knife. I finally went down and looked him over. He was a big bear. After he was salted two or three days, his hide measured eleven foot three inches across from toe to toe.

I found out later when the hunter got back to camp, he told my son a bear killed me. [The hunter] was so shook up, he got out his Seagrams and got drunk. A PenAir plane landed a little later, bringing in another group of clients. That hunter got on the plane and I haven't seen him to this day. I called and asked him if he wanted his bear. No, he didn't want that bear!! I always say, "If you fool around with them bears, you'll have some close calls every once in awhile."

The final expansion of Marlin's guiding activities took him to the northeastern portion of the State, the primary quarry being Dall sheep.

We hunted sheep on the Hula Hula River up in the Arctic National Wildlife Refuge. I knew about that area 'cause I worked with a man who prospected up there. It looked very good for sheep, and that's what I needed. We flew a load of horses into Arctic Village and trailed 'em over the mountains. Turned out we didn't really need 'em 'cause we walked out of camp to get sheep.

We worked two days, getting our camp all set up and everything cleaned up and put away. That evening, we were glassing around. We saw sixty-four full curl or better rams just sitting right there at camp. So, if you've got a population of sheep like that, hell, you don't have to use a damn airplane to go find sheep. We had virtually 100-percent success on our sheep hunting up there, and we wouldn't even hunt the area around camp that much. We saved it for last.

The season would open the minute after midnight on August 10th. At that time of year, you have twenty-four hours of daylight up there. The hunters would get in two days before the season starts. We'd hike around and look it over and pick out some sheep we were gonna hunt. The evening before opening day, we'd get up there and make our stalk. When it got a minute after midnight, we'd shoot a sheep. The hunters couldn't get over that. Their first day of hunting and it's all over for 'em.

Even the last years I hunted there, we took sheep out of that area that were just as good as we had taken at the beginning. Some Fish and Wildlife people told me the sheep numbers are now down about half of what they were when I was there. They attribute the decline to wolf predation. If they don't do something about the wolves, they'll continue taking the sheep numbers down.

And, what's a hunting guide without a Kodiak brown bear story? Marlin has a couple good ones.

One year, we were down deer hunting on Kodiak. We got two nice bucks. I was gonna butcher 'em out right there. We were just getting started and here comes this big old brown bear, and he wasn't gonna leave. I'd holler at him, and I shot underneath of him. Hell, he didn't pay any attention to that at all. Finally, after a big hassle, he started walking off. I figured I'd get these dressed out and get out of there. I was on the last deer, and here comes that damn bear again. The hunter was coming back for another load and he hollered, "That bear's right behind you." So we're going back and forth again, arguing who's gonna keep that deer. Finally he got wind of the other gut pile and he goes over to it. The hunter's got a picture of me dressing out one deer and the bear's right next to me eating on the other gut pile.

I've taken some big bears off of Kodiak. We had one hunter who wanted a big bear. One morning, we got up within 125 yards of a nice bear. He was shooting a .375 and he shot the bear and it took off. He was hit hard, but it didn't knock him down. My assistant guide was carrying a 7mm and I say, "Let him have it." That shot knocked him flat, just rolled him right over. Four of us was pulling on that carcass, and we could not get him up out of there. So we got in the creek and started skinning him. We took the hams and shoulders off, but we still couldn't pull out the torso. We had to finish skinning him in that creek. Of course that meant the hide was soaking wet. We got it on the pack board and me and one of my assistant guides took turns packing. It was getting late and the weather was awful and we're still quite a ways from camp. I told the hunter, "We ain't gonna get stuck in this stuff in the dark." We left that hide on the ridge and came back next morning. The weather was still bad but we made it into camp. We kept telling that guy, "We're just gonna have to cut that hide in two, it's just too heavy to pack." He didn't like that idea. That bear scored an honest ten and a half foot. He's got a life-size mount.

Marlin's tenure as a big game guide spanned many years, many species, many adventures, and many changes. He cherishes the wonderful people he met and the incomparable experiences they have shared.

It's been a good life. I met some very interesting people, and enjoyed most of 'em. A few of 'em, they couldn't come hunting with me again, I don't give a damn how much money they had. I like the outdoors and enjoyed the guiding. I had to make a living anyway and guiding was a good way of spending some of my time outdoors.

My son Eddie was eight years old the first year he packed into my place up there in Boulder Creek. He always lived for the time when he could get out with me. He was dead-set on being a school teacher. That didn't work out, so he came back and hunted with me until we quit. We still go out hunting on our own and have a good time. That's more fun now than when we had to do it for a living.

{MARLIN GRASSER PASSED AWAY IN 2009}

Eastern Interior

Area of detail

Fort Yukon, Nabesna, Gakona,
Healy Lake, Copper Center

RICHARD CARROLL
Fort Yukon, AK

The Carroll family name is well-known in the Fort Yukon area. Richard's story begins with his father 'coming into the country' more than 100 years ago, searching for gold. Instead, he found a different way of life, one based on hunting and trapping. The elder Carroll eventually became the owner of a trading post in Fort Yukon. The Carroll family has played a prominent role in that community for the past 100 years.

My dad came up to Alaska in 1910. He was from a very poor family. They had to sell everything to pay for his passage. He spent the first winter in the Circle area working for "Old Man" Miller. At that time, he was 17 years old. Miller kind of took dad under his wing. That winter dad met a guy named "Black Jack." He was an elderly trapper who supposedly knew the whole area. He talked my Dad into being his partner. Black Jack was gonna make him forget the gold and get rich trapping. They got in a little boat and floated down from Circle to Fort

Yukon. They got an "outfit" from a trader there and went up the Sheenjek River. The cabin they built still stands today. It turned out that Black Jack didn't know anything about trapping and neither did my Dad. They got in an argument over identifying tracks in the snow. The partnership didn't materialize like it was supposed to.

The elder Carroll worked hard and became successful. He evolved from a young trapper into a successful businessman. But nothing in Bush Alaska ever goes smoothly -- there were a few bumps in the road.

My dad moved back into Fort Yukon. At age 27, he started a trading post. He was such a good friend of the local people, all they had to do was give him a good story and he gave a big outfit. Two years later, my dad had to go to the other store in town and give them a line of BS so he could get an outfit to go trap again. He lost everything and had to start over. It was a vicious circle.

By this time, he had learned how to trap and did pretty good at it. During 1930 to 1942, my dad made enough money from trapping to go back in business again. He used to buy fur for Goldstein Company. Him and a little Jewish furbuyer named John Schwegler used to travel together.

Richard got his hunting and trapping skills from his father. He and his brother went on trapping trips with their Father from the time they were young. But things sometimes didn't go as planned -- not all the memories are pleasant.

Dad had three dogs and I remember his lead dog was called Rum. He must have been at least three feet high, about five feet long and two feet wide. My older brother Tommy used to go with Dad. They'd take off from Fort Yukon on a toboggan about five feet long and 16 inches wide. My brother would always tell a story about that heavy toboggan. According to him, he never saw the front of it because he was always behind trying to hold it up and keep it straight. They'd stay out in the woods for two months and come back into town after New Years.

Trapping was different back then. Modern conveniences have changed the experience.

When two trappers meet today we say, "Well, how did it go out in the woods today?"

"Pretty good. I drove 16 miles out the road and put my snow-go off and ran up in the woods and set a few traps."

This is OK, but it isn't really trapping the way I learned ... getting out there and what we call "siwashing" it. We didn't take a tent. We built a spruce bough house to keep warm night after night until we got our 'lines out and then come back into town.

Today, we have a lot of weekend trappers. It's still trapping but it isn't like the old-time trapping where families load up their boats in the fall with all of their gear and food and dogs. They head upriver and we don't see them again until after New Years, unless they run short of groceries. The whole family does not come in until the following May. They'd bring their furs in and the furbuyers would know when they were coming. They'd all have one hell of a party. The trappers would all try to get the furbuyer drunk in those days. It always backfired. The furbuyers caught on and they generally came up with the best deal.

Bush residents are creative, learning how to make do with little in a harsh land. Richard is no different. He wanted hot lunches while on the trail, so he developed a method that allowed for hot food without the time or effort usually required. Not everyone was convinced.

When I was trapping as a teenager, I'd eat my lunch on the trail. I had a can with some kerosene rags in my toboggan. I'd light it, warm my lunch, and I'd eat going across a lake.

One day, a fella saw me as I was crossing the lake where his cabin was located. He couldn't figure it out, "What the hell is coming across this lake? A locomotive or something?" Clouds of smoke were coming up as I was going along. As I drew up closer to him, he called out to me. Pete was a very foul-mouthed individual. After five minutes of cursing me he asked, "What are you doing? Why have you got a fire in the toboggan?"

I said, "I keep my hands warm and I'm eating my lunch."

He went to town and told the story. He told my Dad, "I think your son is cracking up! He builds a fire in his toboggan and he's going along in the woods eating. He won't stop and make a fire like anybody else!" These are some of the stories they have on me up there.

Richard married young and spent many years "living out," i.e., in a cabin away from town. He has many funny stories of the hard way to learn Bush survival and wilderness living. But those tribulations did not detract from their love for the Bush lifestyle.

One time, we were headed back into Fort Yukon at the end of the trapping season. We stopped at lunch time and made a fire out in the woods so that we could make tea. After a while, our dogs became very alert. There's something wrong. The dogs had been tired and all of a sudden their ears are up and they are smelling something. Well, we had our lunch. I thought I heard something but I wasn't sure. We went on down to Fort Yukon.

Part-way back, another guy came along and says, "What the hell were you guys doing up there? Trying to dig that bear out of the hole?"

I says, "What bear?"

He replied, "Well, you built a fire right over it."

I know it's hard to believe. There might be 100,000 square miles out there, but we happened to build our lunch fire over a bear den!

Richard firmly believes in the old-fashioned Bush gear.

I imagine many of you look through outdoor catalogs and you order a lot of stuff like I do. My dad taught me years ago the warmest and the best sleeping material you can get is a good tanned caribou hide. He had a caribou hide outer shell for sleeping. All he had inside was a very thin summer sleeping bag and he could sleep out in a snow bank at 50 below. Caribou hide is the warmest thing there is. A caribou skin will save your life out there in the woods. Only one thing to remember ... keep it dry!

For good footing, make caribou skin booties with the hair inside. That's very, very warm. Today you see bush pilots wearing either a pair of shoe packs or them bunny boots. Twenty-five, 30 years ago you never saw that. All those bush pilots got caribou skin legging boots. That's the warmest. They knew. You freeze your feet off in this other stuff.

In the early days, the area east of Fort Yukon was informally apportioned into adjacent family traplines. It was not competitive, but rather formed a cooperative atmosphere. That era is gone, and Richard misses it. The skills of trapping seem to be dying out as well, and it's hard to bring in a new generation.

If you look on the map today and go up the Porcupine River, there's not a trapper between the Canadian border and Fort Yukon. At one time they used to be every 10 miles apart. The families are gone. The younger generation has no interest in trapping. I do not know why. I've asked the question many times, "Why don't you go out and trap?" It's a vast and beautiful country, but they just won't do it.

In fact, it's so vast around my place I approached one of the furbuyers with an offer. I said, "Do you know anybody in Fairbanks that would want to come out in the woods? I've got everything he would need. Have him come up and spend the winter."

Sure enough, he brings this guy back in. Boy he was gung-ho!! He brought his own snow machine, gas and everything. I said, "Well, I'm glad you're here. I'm gonna take off for five days and I'll be back." When I came back, he had his snow machine and all his stuff packed up. I says, "Where you going?"

He says, "I can't stand it out here. It's too lonesome, too quiet. I miss my girlfriend in town. This isn't the life for me."

I said, "You just got here!"

Richard passed his trapping skills on to his son, and shared many a season with him. Unfortunately, the lure of a paying job took his son away from the trapline.

The last year my son trapped, he got 142 or 143 lynx. He got around 500 bucks apiece for them. I tried to beat him, but I just couldn't quite do it. I got 138. All my boys are out working today. They're making big money, up on the Slope. So I'm sort of left alone.

LENORA CONKLE
Nabesna, AK

LeNora Conkle was born in Idaho near the Snake River. Along with her eight brothers and sisters, LeNora spent as much time outdoors as she could.

I was the oldest of nine children. We couldn't afford fishing poles but we'd still catch fish. I had all kinds of pets. Skating and swimming were our main hobbies as kids.

I almost drowned when I was ten years old. My brother swam across a canal. He assumed I could follow him. He said, "Oh come on. You ain't gonna drown." Well, I almost did. He turned me upside down on the bank and pumped the water out of me. I didn't how he knew to do that, but it worked. My mother never did know how close I come to drowning. We never told on each other. We never told on anybody.

LeNora married at 16 after graduating from high school and moved to Seattle, but the marriage failed.

It didn't last, so I moved to San Diego. My daughter had a horse. She and her two brothers could not stay on its back. One day, we picked up this Marine and gave him a ride to base in San Diego. Bud came by when my kids would go riding. That wild horse didn't even attempt to shake him. We became good friends and it seemed like he was always around the house.

My brother went to Alaska to work on the fishing boats. I was brokenhearted. I thought I should be able to go too, but I had to stay home. When the war was over, the Marine came back. I said, "Yes, I'll marry you. We'll go to Alaska."

Bud and Lenora drove up the Alaska Highway in 1946. It was the start of a long, adventurous life for the couple.

Bud took my car and traded it for a civilian Jeep to drive the highway. The road was fresh-built and not paved. We followed in the footsteps of the Army.

Both of us got good jobs right off the bat as soon as we got to Fairbanks. The weather wasn't too different than Idaho. It was cold in winter and hot in the summer. I could always stand the cold better than hot, so it didn't bother me. It still doesn't.

With the wages we'd make in town, we'd buy all kinds of camping gear and an aluminum canoe. Every weekend, Bud and I would take our Jeep and go as far away as we could, looking around for a place we liked. We also had a dog team we traipsed around the country with. The dogs would not work for me. They would work for Bud, but they would rather laugh at me. I wasn't too happy with the dogs.

The Conkles eventually found the place they wanted to settle – a mountain lake which suited their needs and fit their definition of "paradise." They built a lodge which served as the base for their guiding operation (both hunting and fishing). They welcomed clients from around the world. Those were rewarding years for the family.

We bought some property on Tanada Lake in the Wrangell Mountains. The lake was six miles long and 1 mile wide. The first camp we had was a tent. We cut logs and floated them across the lake where we built our hunting and fishing lodge.

While we were building the lodge, we were sleeping in tents. The kitchen was a tent and our bedroom was a tent. We built the main part of the kitchen and lodge all out of logs. We had that finished by the time Colin was born. Then we started needing sleeping cabins. Every time we'd get the logs up a certain height, that kid was climbing those logs. He was one little monkey.

We applied for a 160-acre homestead on the Tok Cut-Off. We started a ranch. We had 13 horses. We had plenty of clients willing to take the horses and then some that were not familiar with horses and they would fly in to the lodge.

Bud took lessons to get his pilot's license. I was planning on getting a pilot's license too. I went to the doctor for a physical.

My doctor says, "You can't. You're pregnant."

I hemmed and hawed, "I'm too old."

"No, you're not," he replied.

So I didn't get my license, but I knew I could handle the plane if I had to. Instead, I wrote "Bush Pilot Wives," which explained what we did at home while our men were hunting and fishing and flying.

We bought a Super Cub from Bud's moose hunting partner. It didn't take long to get busy once we got the airplane. We started out flying lots of Fairbanks people in for hunting and fishing. They would usually stay for a week. In order to attract more clients, we advertised in magazines. We also depended on word of mouth. Within two years, we had hunters from all over.

I was the cook. We ate good. You would just throw a line in the water and you had a grayling. We had fresh lake trout out of the lake. We had salmon out of what we called Fish Creek. We also ate caribou, moose, and sheep. Bud was never one to kill anything that he couldn't eat. If we didn't need it, we didn't kill it. I like that spirit.

Our guiding business was just sheep and bear. We had good Dall sheep. We hired guides. Bud was pretty strict with his guides. He made them backpack the client's sheep down the mountain, rather than rolling it down like some people did. One year, we had some cowboys from Wyoming. They wouldn't let those guides carry their rams down off the mountain. The hunters packed it themselves. They were pretty popular with Bud.

There were some clients that were real nice and some that we didn't care for. I can always get along with people, regardless. Bud was more short-tempered. Mostly, we had good happy clients. The bad years were when the clients didn't get their animals. Usually, it was their own fault. They wouldn't work at it or they wanted a bigger animal than the one they shot.

Everyone in Alaska has a good bear story or two. The Conkles are no different.

I didn't hunt, but I decided I was going to learn to be a guide. I'd watch the other guides real close and learn how they handled the grizzly bears. They are not afraid of those bears. They know how to back away if they had a problem. That was the main thing, it seemed like. I met face-to-face with a grizzly bear at the ranch and he backed up. We'd always watch for bears when we would go berry picking. I never was afraid of the grizzly bears.

We had trouble with the bears at the lodge. We had a log cabin and the bears would either pull the doors off or break the windows. One old bear slept the whole winter on Bud's bed. He ate all the pillows. He ate all the canned goods. It tore up everything but my Bible. Bud was mad at that bear and said he would shoot it if he could find the right one.

In addition to being chief cook, Lenora was also chief transportation officer. She drove many hours and miles hauling supplies and getting clients to and from the lodge in her family station wagon.

I was usually the one who drove into Anchorage to pick up the hunters. Sometimes, I'd get tired and let the clients drive. Some of them drove like they did back home on freeways. I'd make up some excuse to get the wheel back again.

A gal from Gulkana often went with me. That was our lady's fun … buying the groceries. We wouldn't let the boys at the market pack our station wagon. There were lots of bumps on the road, so you had to know how to pack things so they wouldn't break.

Our son Colin was driving our truck when he was twelve. One time, we had three clients come in to Gulkana. We sent Colin with the truck to pick them up. We told him to let one of the clients drive back. The clients couldn't believe he drove the truck.

Lenora admits the remote lodge was more Bud's dream than hers, but she grew to love it too. Throughout their tenure in the guiding business, Lenora most enjoyed meeting the various people who visited their lodge.

When Bud and I came to Alaska to start our dream of the hunting lodge, we were both near 40. I didn't think I'd still be here 60 years later. Alaska is a land that draws people and you are not disappointed. Unfortunately, so many women won't stay.

We came up here with a spirit of adventure. The lodge was Bud's dream and it came true for him. He talked me into it, and it wasn't too bad. What I liked best was all the people that I met.

Of all the places I've been, Tanada Lake is my favorite place. It was home. I loved the wilderness.

{LENORA CONKLE PASSED AWAY IN 2013}

TOR HOLMBOE

Gakona, AK

Tor Holmboe was born and raised in Norway. His family had a large commercial operation harvesting seals and polar bears. As a young man, he grew frustrated with the government and left the country.

Back then, Tromso was an isolated place. We didn't have any connection with the outside world except our ferry boat. In the wintertime, we were snowed in and left in the dark. That was the environment where I grew up.

Our family had three sealing vessels. The seals were taken with a rifle, on the east coast of Greenland and also in waters off northern Russian. My father had a trapping station at the south end of the Spitsbergen Island. There was an annual migration of 1,500 polar bears across that island. Our biggest catch in any one winter was 144 polar bears.

I joined the Norwegian State Police right after World War II. They were building up an entirely new force following the Nazi occupation. I was patrolling on the Russian Arctic border as a member of the ski patrol. To my big disappointment, that duty was turned over to the Army. We were shipped south and faced with a different sort of duty I had not anticipated. I resigned from the force.

I was waiting for an excuse to leave the country. When the Socialist Party was re-elected, I decided I didn't want to wait another four years for that to change so I came to the United States.

Tor arrived in the United States in 1954. He moved to the Territory of Alaska a few years later. He worked as a commercial fisherman until he could purchase his own boat for salmon and crab.

The first time I came up to Alaska, it was as a combination cook and deck-hand on a company tender to Seldovia. I got acquainted with a lot of commercial fishermen. Later on, the opportunity presented itself to come back on a more permanent basis. I came North and have been here ever since.

Fisheries management has changed a lot in Alaska. Prior to statehood the salmon were harvested to a large degree by company-owned fish traps. After statehood, the traps were outlawed and the harvest of fish was done by individual fishermen. I saw the opportunity to start as a salmon fisherman which I did for 20-some years. In the fall, I also fished king crab out of Kodiak.

One day while reading the paper, Tor found an article about a woman trapper. He contacted the woman under (mildly) false pretenses, but all was forgiven when they met. They married soon thereafter. Thus began Tor's life as a trapper.

One winter, I was reading a copy of the Anchorage Times. The headline said "The Trapper is a Lady." I read about this woman who had her trapline on the Yukon River 55 miles below Eagle. Her food supply had spoiled. She had quite a hard time that winter, spending most of her time hunting for food in addition to trapping. It was a long article with the picture of this beautiful woman. I thought that is one I should get in touch with.

I wrote her a letter and came up here before fishing started that summer. I went back to Cook Inlet and did my salmon season and returned up here in August. We were married and went down the Yukon. That was the beginning of my trapping career, which turned into quite an adventure. My wife taught me everything she knew about trapping.

Tor and Norma trapped the Yukon 'line on foot for many years. They were perfectly happy with their simple life.

Our cabin was built by an old-timer back in 1917. His name was Jim Taylor. It was such a beautiful cabin. That Jim Taylor had a way of living in the woods. There were a lot of innovations you don't see every day. He had a log drying house where he let the dogs dry out after they had been in the overflow. He had a log whelping cabin for the females. He had a wood railroad from way back in the woods where he got his firewood. He built a wooden flat-car with wooden wheels. He would load the flat-car with firewood and his dog team would pull it into his cabin. He also had a wooden boat launch to launch his riverboat. He left information about his trapping system, complete with trap locations and campsites all marked on a map.

Jim Taylor was an excellent trapper. One year during the depth of the Depression, he took out over $20,000 worth of fur when people were searching high and low for a dollar. Unfortunately, he had one big problem. He was a compulsive gambler. He would take his winter's catch over to Dawson City or Fort Yukon and sell it. The next stop would be the card house and he would lose all his money. This repeated itself year after year. When he passed away in 1937, he was penniless. My wife found out about the cabin. She bought it for $200. I still have the bill of sale. Very little was needed in line of repairs.

Over the years, Taylor cleared out a lot of trails in the area and marked them with good blazes. I think he could have run the trails blindfolded, but I certainly benefited from the blazes. One year, I was walking one of the trails and found a crumbly old wolf snare attached to a wooden drag. It was in a place that gave no indication of being a good spot for anything. As I mentioned, Jim Taylor was a very skilled trapper, so the discovery of that snare was valuable information. I remember saying, "Well Jim, if you say so." I had a #4 Thompson snare in my pack. I cut a new drag and replaced the old snare with my new snare. I put a few twigs here and there and stepped back and looked at it. I wasn't too impressed by what I saw. I walked by that snare numerous times, without catching anything. Then one day, I came to that snare spot and there was the biggest wolf I've ever seen. It was my first wolf.

Like other trappers before him, Tor preferred the old ways to the new. He chose to travel his 'line via ski rather than snowmachine.

We trapped on foot, on skis and snowshoes. We didn't have snowmachines; that came later. Skis were my favorite. I would cover 20 miles per day. In fact, I wore out a pair of skis one winter. I don't know how many miles I put on those skis. That was a very good way of traveling in the woods.

Eventually, the temptation to get motorized was too much to resist so we got snowmachines. With good hindsight, we would have been better off to continue on skis. I think the bottom line would be practically the same. With skis, we didn't have the expenses of acquiring a machine and keeping it running. The noise and the smell of the machine contributed to less cash per mile than I did on skis.

And snowmachines often break down.

My wife had some dramatic happenings. One time is worth mentioning. She had left the cabin on her snowmachine to check traps. I was working in the yard and she comes walking. She had her trapping basket on and she was pretty tuckered out so I knew she had walked quite a little distance.

I said, "What happened?"

She said, "You're not going to like this."

I said, "Could you give me a hint?"

She said, "You need help. The snowmachine is in water."

She had caught an otter at a place we called Otter Lake. She could not sit down and pull the starter cord. She wasn't strong enough for that. So she was standing beside the machine and pulling the cord when it started. The throttle was stuck. The machine took off on its own.

She said, "I have never before prayed and hoped it would hit a tree, but I did that time."

Unfortunately, it missed everything. It went over a 15-foot embankment and nose first into 6 feet of water with the engine running. I took block and tackle, come-along, chain saw, and everything else I could think of. When I got there, the tail end was floating. I had to build kind of a dock so I could work off of it. I had to turn the machine around in the water because the skis would hang up on the dead trees in the beaver dam.

I rigged up a line to a tree on top of this 15-foot embankment. With the block and tackle and my come-along, I got it out of there. After I got it out, I left all my equipment where it was. I just hooked up her machine to mine and ran it home. Four bolts held the engine in that little machine. Took it out and brought it inside. It was just beginning to slush up. It would have busted had I had not done that. We emptied out the water. Between hundreds of pulls and a couple of cans of WD-40, I managed to dry it out in about a week. I put the engine back in the machine and it ran better than ever. She had to ride on a frozen seat the rest of the winter, but at least it ran.

Norma had a well-deserved reputation as an excellent cook.

My wife used to bake bread in a drum oven that we inserted in the smoke stack. It's similar to a stack robber. It's a double-wall oven and the smoke can travel on the outside. She could bake two loaves at a time and it did a good job. The way she regulated the heat in the oven was by the draft on the stove.

She got a job one time. She had heard about a prospecting camp a few miles off the road that didn't have a cook. She strapped that same oven on her pack-board and hiked in there. She said, "I heard you needed a cook." The main geologist said "No, we didn't really, but since you walked all this way, we'll hire you." For $15 a day, she became their camp cook.

One winter, the Holmboes trapped in the Wrangell Mountains. Tor had an interesting encounter with a Dall sheep.

There was a trail that connected Ptarmigan Lake with Rock Lake. There were a lot of wolf tracks in the area. So I placed a trap in a wolf trail. One day, there was a full-grown sheep in the trap. It wasn't badly hurt, so I wanted to release it. I decided to approach it backwards because I didn't want to be pounded in the front. I worked my way up to the sheep and wrestled it down. It was quite a job.

I could see the fright in that animal's eyes and its heart was going 100 miles an hour. I started talking to it calmly and scratching it behind the ears. Before long, that sheep laid his head in my hand like a dog would do. The fear disappeared from its eyes. He was just laying there. I worked the trap off of its hoof and stood up. The sheep was still lying there, so I say, "Hey sheep ... get up." Eventually he stood and shook himself. I said, "Get on your way." He turned around and walked away.

Tor and Norma lived on the Tok Cut-Off for many years. Wildlife was abundant. Tor noticed changes in animal populations. Like many Alaskans, he has an opinion as to the reasons for the changes.

We used to get a moose very year, but not anymore. We never needed a whole moose anyway. We split one with one or two of the neighbors. It worked both ways. If I got one, I shared it with them. If they got one, they shared it with me.

In the early days, moose were really thick here in the Slana area. You could look out the window any day in the winter-time and at least see signs of moose. We had them look in through the window at night and bed down in the trail to the outhouse. Now, you don't see a track here. The three main reasons for that are:
- wolves in the wintertime,
- bears at calving time (it seems like bears go on a moose calf diet),
- potlatch harvest by the local Natives; that has been devastating.

In the early days, caribou was no big deal either. We were allowed three caribou and it was not a matter of IF we got them. It was a matter of WHEN we got them. They'd track right through the yard here, so we waited until they "knocked on the door." They still do that to some extent but things change. Nothing stays the same.

We've had bears that tried to get into our bedroom window and we've had wet bear tracks on the porch in the morning; both blacks and grizzlies. My wife quit counting after she shot 15, and that was many years ago.

They were mostly blacks. The blacks can be nasty. It was a black that tried to crawl in through the bedroom window.

Our dog woke her up one night. That dog had a very definite bear bark. It meant "BEAR" with capital letters. I was away from home. She jumped out of bed and ran outside in her pajamas. The bear took off around the corner of the house with the dog in hot pursuit. My wife went the other way. The bear and my wife met at the opposite corner. She didn't have time to raise her gun. She just burnt one off from the hip. The bear took off and the feet were moving like a buzz saw trying to get away.

There have been other close encounters. I was attacked by a bear about six miles from here. It was a very nasty situation. In the spring of the year, I went to check on a moose carcass left by wolves the previous winter. I left the trail and walked about 200 yards down to the carcass. I had to get close in order to see it because of the brush. I was only about 20 yards away when the carcass came into view. It was freshly covered with wet moss. I took the gun off my back and released the safety. The bear appeared, just like that. He had been sleeping. He came at me. I raised my gun and realized I made a bad mistake and left the scope on. You don't do that in thick brush. A scope is useless in the brush. So I thought, "You're just going to have to come as close as you can where I can't miss." That bear was three steps away from me when I burnt one off. He went down like a ton of bricks and never got back up.

Tor served a brief tenure on the local Fish and Game Advisory Committee, an experience which he found less than satisfying. He's not very fond of the Alaska National Interest Lands Conservation Act (ANILCA) which created a multitude of new national Parks and Preserves.

I was on the local Fish & Game Advisory Committee for a few years. We tried to define subsistence use. We spent three years trying, but we gave up. We could not come up with a definition that was acceptable to the authorities.

The Park Service is doing their job. They have some very good people, but the existence of the Park is a step backwards for anybody who has lived off the land the way it used to be. I think they went overboard when they designated so much of Alaska as parks.

All in all, Tor has loved his life in the Last Frontier, with Norma and the traplines and the wildlife.

The biggest value of an outdoor lifestyle is therapeutic. With a trapline no longer than we had (40 or 50 miles), the best we could do was break even, but that was OK with us. We lived very comfortably in the wintertime. We did what we wanted to do.

Most of all, we enjoyed a very healthy lifestyle, without any stress. We weren't hung up on "hurry to do this, hurry to do that." We used the signs we saw in the woods, tried to come up with an idea or answer. Sometimes we hit it right and most of the times we didn't. I made so many wolf sets which I KNEW would work, only to come back and find them empty. But nothing depended on that.

Of course, it was rewarding for us to out-fox the wolves, but the therapeutic value of trapping was the big thing. My wife … same thing. She spent the happiest times of her life on the trapline.

I'm 80 years old now, and it's all behind me.

{TOR HOLMBOE PASSED AWAY IN 2011}

PAUL KIRSTEATTER

Healy Lake, AK

Paul Kirsteatter grew up on a ranch in New Mexico. He came to Alaska, courtesy of Uncle Sam, and made it his permanent home. He married an Indian woman from the village of Healy Lake.

When I was a kid I liked to trap coyotes. A government trapper would go through the ranch country on a horse taking coyotes. I followed him around. I came up to Alaska here in '43 in the service. I left in the spring of '45, but turned around and come right back up.

My wife's parents died when she was two years old. She was raised by her grandparents who didn't speak English. She knew all the old ways, which made it a lot easier for me. Rather than me learning by experience, she already knew most of the methods. She was an expert trapper, an expert skin sewer, could run boats, shoot her own moose, run fish nets, and all the rest. The old timers were honorable people. Their livelihood depended on understanding the behavior of wildlife. Many of our biologists could gain knowledge if they would [listen] to them.

We usually had about 25 dogs; big work, dogs. I used 10 to 12 dogs on the trapline. My wife had a team, too. She could also skin a lot of animals I trapped. She traveled on the trapline with me. Two of my kids were born right on the trapline. When we traveled from one camp to another, my wife would throw the kids in a sleeping bag on the dog sled.

During the summer, [we] had snares to build, sleds to build and dog harnesses to get ready. I was fortunate because the family pretty well took care of the chores and I had the freedom to go hunting and prospecting. I could be gone for a month or two at a time and I never worried about the family. They took care of themselves pretty well. I tried to cut up all the firewood ahead of time for the main camps. This gave me more time for trapping during the winter time.

We put up a lot of fish, not only smoked fish for us to eat but several tons of dried fish for the dogs. We also put up a lot of dried meat — caribou and moose. We had big gardens. The whole family worked and contributed to making a living out there. That's what it takes if you're going to make a living trapping. It would be pretty tough now, although it could be done if you had good trapping country, a lot of fur and everybody in the family worked at it.

Paul's family ran dog teams for trapline transportation and to haul supplies. Paul credits the dogs with keen senses and a tireless work ethic. The dogs weren't pleased when Paul exchanged their pulling power for a snowmachine, and sent a clear message showing their contempt.

We depended on dogs, not only for trapping but for hauling in wood and supplies. I must give my wife a lot of credit. It takes a lot of work to care for dogs. You have to be good to them if you're going depend on them.

When you run a dog team on the trapline, the wolves are more comfortable running your trail. Once you start catching wolves in the trail, then they associate those trails with danger and they quit running them.

The first snow machine I bought was in 1974. The big advantage of a snow machine is you can cover a lot of country. I remember when I retired my dogs. Every time my lead dog got loose, he'd make a bee-line to that snow machine and raise his leg. Another time, the snow machine ran out of gas. I was about 20 miles from home, so I had to snowshoe all the way home. I hooked the dogs up to the sled, and took some gas out to the machine. The dogs wet it down all the way around.

My wife didn't like the machines very well. One day, I had the snow machine in the shop. I was tightening some bolts to adjust the track.

She says, "What are you doing down there? You're supposed to be checking your 'line."

I told her, "I'm just tightening up the nuts."

She said, "You don't have to tighten the nuts on those dogs."

The overflow on the rivers can get you in a lot of trouble. With a dog team, when your lead dog got in snow that had overflow underneath, he'd usually stop and look back at you. If you were smart you found another way around. With machines, you often break through and then you're real trouble, especially if it's real cold weather.

Wolves were a primary focus for Paul. He trapped them in the winter. He took pups out of dens in the summer. The pups were sometimes used for scientific study. Some were held in captivity to breed with sled dogs.

I raised wolves, too. I experimented with a lot of baits and lures to get their reaction. I also sold wolves to local people and several universities. I tried unsuccessfully to cross them with dogs. I learned when they reach breeding age, the wolf killed the dog.

Digging wolves out of dens is a two man job. I usually spent the months of May and June at it, and covered a lot of country in the Fortymile looking for dens. We got quite good at it. Each of us would have two dogs packing our gear. Wolves hate dogs. When dogs got close to the den, the adult wolves would go after them and you had a chance to shoot the adult wolves.

Some of those dens had been hunted for many years. The wolves become real smart and hid their dens. If we could get within five miles of a den, we could locate it. We'd set up a lookout across the valley where you could see a game trail. Wolves usually hunt at night. If you saw wolves traveling early in the morning, you could be pretty sure they were going back to their den. That told you the direction of the den. We'd also wipe out tracks in the mud at creek crossings and on game trails. You'd check those spots twice a day (morning and evening) to determine which way the wolves were traveling.

Wolves are like dogs in a lot of ways. When he wakes up and starts moving around, he's got to relieve himself. So, you find wolf scat along the trail. As the piles got more numerous, you were getting closer to the den. The entire pack would be working to feed that year's pups. When the adults feed, they come back to the den and puke it up in piles. The pups will come out and gorge on this stuff the adults have disgorged.

The dogs also helped when you got closer to the den. The dogs would let out a low cry. If you'd listen real careful, you could hear the pups answer. Even if we didn't hear it, the dogs would and they'd make a straight line to the den.

When we knew there were pups in a den, it was time to start digging. One guy would stand guard and the other guy would go into the den. The tunnel going into the den was fairly narrow. A man had to get sideways to crawl in. We used to take a little shovel and a gunny sack which had lines on two corners. The guy that goes inside shovels dirt into the gunny sack. The partner outside pulls it out and dumps it and then you pull it back inside. You keep that up 'til you get back to where the pups are.

I recall one time going into a den. I had a flashlight ahead of me. I glanced up and there's an adult female right in front of me, snarling. I made a fast retreat out of there. My partner said I came out backwards faster than he had ever seen. I borrowed his .30-30, crawled back in there, and shot the bitch in the den. Then I couldn't hear anything for about three weeks. We had to use sign language. I learned you don't shoot a high-powered rifle inside of a den without plugging your ears.

The most pups I ever took out of a single den was nine or ten. Usually it's five. Younger wolves don't have that many pups but the older wolves do. One time in the Fortymile country, my partner and I found two dens right together, about 20 feet apart. We took 22 pups out of those two dens, plus we got most of the older wolves.

Paul has trapped in Alaska since 1946, so he's seen the good years and the bad years.

There were years when things were pretty slim. We concentrated on furs that were worth some money. I used to do real good on lynx. There's been years when I caught over 100. There have also been years when the price was so low they weren't worth skinning.

In other years, I concentrated on beaver. I was fortunate to have hundreds and hundreds of lakes and ponds where there were beaver. At one time in the late 1940s, a beaver hide was worth $1 an inch. Wolf hides weren't worth too much, but we got the bounty, which was $50 a head. You'd starve to death on that today, but $50 would buy you some beans in those years.

Some years, I concentrated on marten. Right after World War II, we were getting $110 a piece for black marten. Those years, I trapped in the high country of the Fortymile which is noted as one of the best marten areas in Alaska. I did real well there. Then by the early 1950s, the price of marten had gone down to nothing, partly because the Russians were shipping in sable. They flooded the market and the price of marten went down to $4 or $5.

I had a run-in with a wolverine one time. I was running my 'line with a dog team. The wolverine was in a trap up ahead. A dog knows for 100 yards when you've got something ahead in a trap. The dogs might be moping along and all at once they pick up and start running. You know there's something up there in a trap. In this particular instance, it was real cold weather. The dogs put on a burst of speed. I saw an animal up there and I jumps on the brake with both feet. I used a one- inch rope to tie the sled to a spruce tree about four inches in diameter.

As I walked up to the wolverine, I pulled out my pistol and was ready to shoot him. Out of the corner of my eye, I saw a dog on either side of me. They'd all hit that tow line so hard they snapped off that tree because it was brittle from the cold. The dogs ran by on both sides of me, knocked me down and ended up on top of the wolverine. The next thing I saw was a wolverine a foot in front of my face. I back-tracked out of there real fast. The dogs were all in one pile on top of the wolverine. I grabbed a dog by the tail, pulled him back, and whacked him on the nose with a new ax handle I carried on the sled. I pulled one dog after the other off the wolverine. When I got down toward the bottom of the pile, the wolverine had my biggest dog by the nose. That wolverine chewed up and ruined two of my dogs. When I skinned that wolverine out, he never even had a hole in him.

In the early years, I used tent camps. Those are not too comfortable when it's 50 below. Whenever I got a chance, I built a ten foot by 12 foot shelter out of logs. I made them low, with no windows; Yukon stove, bunk across the back. Used a kerosene light, just enough so you could cook your meal and skin fur. For a door, I used the tarp off the sled. Traveling by dog team, you needed a shelter like that every 15 or 20 miles. When you ran into trouble, like bad weather or overflow on the river, you needed shelter close by. The tents worked for awhile, but they're not the best when you get cold weather.

Paul was widely known as a man who understood wolf behavior and used that knowledge to trap the wild canines.

I used mostly snares for wolves. Occasionally, I used traps. My best luck was to use "gang" sets of multiple snares in a thicket. I once caught 17 wolves in one gang set. It took me awhile to get them home. They were all frozen in different poses. Try to get them onto a dog sled and then get down the trail and through the brush. Then it would take three days of slow heat in a cabin to thaw them out. When they started thawing out, it sure clears your sinuses. And a small cabin doesn't give you a lot of room for thawing. Wolf trapping is not easy.

Predator control is a controversial issue in today's world. Paul firmly believes in the need for predator control when circumstances dictate. However, he is adamantly opposed to the use of poison, having witnessed the negative effects of federal poison programs prior to statehood.

Back in the 1950s, Fish and Wildlife Service used poison to kill wolves. They'd have a bag of seal oil pellets with the 1080 poison. They'd drop a quarter of a caribou or moose. Then they'd circle back and drop that bag, which would hit the ground and scatter the pellets around. Wolves were supposed to gallop up there and eat the pellets. I have pictures of dead marten, fox, and ravens ... everything but wolves. The Fish and Wildlife Service was telling us their baits were selective. They were not selective. It kills every animal that'll eat bait. Enough of us trappers out there in the woods saw the effects of that program. We don't ever want to see something like that here in Alaska again. ANY kind of predator control is better than that.

We have to have some sort of predator control if we're going have enough game for the people who depend on it. You hear people talk about a "balance of nature." They claim wolves take only sick and weak animals. Truly, they do take some of the sick and weak, but in the middle of winter I haven't seen any pack of wolves that couldn't bring down the healthiest moose. There is no such thing as a "balance of nature." By controlling predators and controlling the take of game, humans can make more of a balance than letting nature take care of itself. Nature is a big waster. In times of surplus, lots of animals aren't harvested. They usually starve during winters or get killed by predators.

Paul adopted Alaska as his home, and lived an adventurous, satisfying life. He'd live no other place, no other way.

I've only been Outside one time since I moved up here and that was to Seattle. I don't have no desire to go back Outside. Alaska's been good to me. I've raised a family. They all know how to make a living. I love the outdoors and it's been a good life.

{PAUL KIRSTEATTER PASSED AWAY IN 2012, JUST SHY OF HIS 90TH BIRTHDAY}

DEAN WILSON
Northway, AK

Dean Wilson grew up in the eastern Interior village of Northway. Most people lived a traditional subsistence lifestyle. Money and jobs were scarce. Native elders taught him necessary skills, such as making dog sleds, snowshoes, and canoes. While acknowledging the hardships, Wilson has fond memories of the simple life he knew as a child.

When I was young, it was a really good era. People lived a much simpler lifestyle. Everybody struggled for existence. People had to figure a way to make a living off of the land. Trapping was one way people made a living and hunting was another. There were a few hunting guides. All in all, it was a pretty tough life.

I never remember going hungry, but I remember eating a lot of beans and a lot of pancakes for an extended period of time. Muskrat trapping was a very big activity. People ate a lot of muskrats. It wasn't considered a delicacy, but it was considered everyday table fare. Ducks and geese, they were very important too. They did a whole variety of things to catch fish. Life was difficult, but it was adventuresome.

You had to learn to think a little differently. You couldn't think about money because money wasn't important. What you thought of was, "What is there to feed us here?" That was very important in people's minds then because times were tough.

I still do a lot of reminiscing about the old days when things were much simpler. I didn't have much appreciation for it then, but I do now.

Dog teams were used daily, and were important for most seasonal activities, a vital component to living and thriving off the land.

Dogs were an important part of the early lifestyle, and dogs have almost been forgotten. They were such an asset in that period of time. A man with well-trained, obedient dogs had a big advantage over the person that didn't have that going for him. They were an important tool for survival in the country.

We would use them to scent in on a den site or to help guard against bears at night when people were at camp sleeping. People used them to haul whatever they needed -- a sled-load of wood, ice or snow for water, and equipment. The dogs were used a lot in the summers to pack a load, too. When people were out hunting, they would take dogs to pack the groceries and maybe a sleeping bag. The dogs were certainly an asset during hunting season. They did most of the packing. People would shoot a moose and make camp right there – move their camp to the kill. They would stay there for however long it would take to dry the meat. Then they would walk out – two or three dogs could pack a whole moose if it's dried up. You can drop that weight down to nothing by drying it.

Harvesting furbearers for income didn't always involve the use of traps.

In the 1940s, people didn't keep cars running in the winter. The only way to keep a car warm was to have a garage. We lived in 12 foot by 12 foot cabins, so the men were not going to take the time to build adequate garages for the cars, as well. When the lynx cycle was very high, my dad and some other men in Northway would get a car running and hunt lynx at night. At that time, almost every vehicle had spotlights on the side. You could look way ahead with your spotlight. If they were lucky, they might get half a dozen lynx in one night.

Walter Northway was the chief, and the village was named after him. He was an incredible hunter.

Walter knew animal habits so well he could predict if you spooked a moose it would go here or there, and be reasonably accurate. He also was a very good shot. He was a man of great wisdom in living off the country. He was a real good teacher, and he enjoyed teaching kids. No matter what my little brother Leroy and I would be doing (maybe shooting squirrels with a sling shot or making a bow and arrow or skinning muskrats) Walter would come by and he would always stop and help you – show you a better way of doing things. He was a kind, gentle man. He really liked to interact with the kids. He always was good at passing on things. He was the best bow maker. He was, without question, the best snowshoe maker. He was really good at all those things – canoes and boats and rifles. He was a leader by example.

Walter had a younger brother named Steven. For some reason, Steven and I clicked. I remember one time when I was fishing in the creek. He just come over and sat down and talked to me for two or three hours. I think that day we were talking about building a canoe. Everybody had a canoe in those days and mostly you built them. Steven talked to me about how to do it. I'm not sure of all the details now, but that was the Indian way of teaching.

People in the village started with nothing and made something out of it – made a sled or a pair of snowshoes or a canoe. The one tool I saw used more than anything else by the older people was a good axe. I've seen people do amazing things with an old Swede saw and an axe.

Dean and his brothers started trapping when they were seven or eight years old, inheriting their love of and skills in trapping from their father. But trapping wasn't the only lesson imparted by Wilson's dad. He remembers the sense of pride he got when using his hard-earned fur check to purchase practical items, rather than wasting it on frivolity.

My dad loved to trap and a lot of that rubbed off on me. I was thrilled whenever I got to go on a trapline with my dad. Me and my brothers trapped squirrels and muskrats mostly. Johnny Schwegler ("Muskrat Johnny," we called him) would come around two or three times a year to buy fur. When we knew Johnny was coming, we checked all our traps and got everything skinned and ready to market. Us kids always knew to go there before your dad and him started talking business. He'd give us an extra quarter per hide. Once we sold those hides, we weren't allowed to just go spend that money. Our parents exerted control over that. We were supposed to use that money for clothes or useful things. I paid for my first fishing pole with fur money. Boy, that was neat!!

Even the most skilled outdoorsman can be tripped up by Nature's hazards, and Wilson was no exception, He encountered many dangers during his years on the trapline, most noteworthy being those near misses with weak ice on fast-flowing rivers.

One time, I fell through the ice up to my knees and got wet. The training I got from being around the Indian people came to my rescue. We were taught what to do if you get your feet wet. You go to the nearest grove of spruce trees, take a long stick, and knock down a squirrel nest. Pull out all that little fine nesting material they use, which is nothing more than good dry grasses. Take your boot off and wipe everything as dry as you can. Take your sock off and wipe your foot as dry as you can. Pack grass on the bottom of your boot for an insole, put your foot in, and then pack a layer of dry grass around your feet. Those Native people were full of little tricks of the trade in survival situations.

One year, we had a poor freeze-up. We got a lot of cold weather early and then we had a couple feet of snow. I can "read" ice pretty good, but it was very hard to read the ice that year. I was breaking trail and I had to make a crossing in a place that I didn't like. When I was headed home, I had to go the same way and it was long after dark. I had cardinal rule – you never travel on ice after dark. That cardinal rule got broken a whole lot of times, but it was a good rule and it should have been obeyed this time!

As I reached the crossing, I had to go over a little bit of a crest and then down into a little bit of a slump in the ice. As I looked ahead, I could see a dark spot. Something didn't look right, so I swerved off to the side at the last second. The dark spot was open water. I just barely kept my snow machine from going in that open hole. The water wasn't too deep, but it was really fast. Fast-moving water can sweep you off your feet and you go down and start kissing the ice from the bottom side. That ain't good!

Wilson was widely recognized as a hard-working trapper, so he was mildly miffed when a less-energetic trapper said he was just "lucky."

A friend often commented about how lucky I was on the trapline. After hearing that comment several times, I got to thinking about that. I had out over 300 big traps, plus lots of snares. This other guy had about an eight-mile long 'line. I could go by his house almost any day of the week and catch him at home. At my place, you had to wait until seven at night, if I was even there by then. If I was there, most nights I would be skinning. My "luck" always seemed to run in direct proportion to the amount of sets I kept working.

Wilson got into the furbuying business almost reluctantly. He developed Klondike Alaska Furs into a successful enterprise, and earned a reputation for honesty. He remembers the people he worked with while buying furs, and enjoys the memories, but sometimes wonders, "what if" he'd kept trapping instead.

My father bought furs at his trading post, [so] I had a basic understanding of quality of furs and marketing basics. Other local trappers would ask me where I was selling furs, what price I was getting. At that time, I was doing a little better than what they were able to do selling to the local furbuyers. Some of them asked me to include their furs with mine. This went on for a couple of years and then some of the guys were saying I should just buy the furs from them and then sell them for whatever I could get. I started doing that for them, and from there it just evolved! I never intended to buy fur, it wasn't my goal, but I finally started to do more and more of it.

Furbuying is a different kind of game. It's really a good way of life, but the trappers are always pretty sure they're getting had. If you're paying $100 each for a squirrel, you'd have some guy that would moan and groan about it and swear up and down that if you send them squirrels to outer Mongolia you'd get $200 for them. That's the way it goes.

I met a lot of really nice people. A lot of down-to-earth, homespun people who were doing exactly what they wanted to be doing and they enjoyed it. Furbuying wasn't bad, but I sometimes think I would have been happier just staying on the trapline.

Cabins are crucial to the survival and success of a long-line trapper, and Wilson was no exception. He developed and refined a system for building simple shelters -- not works of art, but providing a warm place at the end of a long day on the 'line.

One of the first cabins I worked on was actually a rebuilding job. The roof caved in and the floor had kinda buckled. I rebuilt that cabin to the point it was usable. The original walls had been built without any nails. They used an auger-type drill, bored holes in each log, and pegged it to the log below. We worked on it for a number of days. You couldn't help but ache to hear the stories of the people who built it and the people who used it over the years. It still stands today, and is still usable.

My brother-in-law and I decided to put a cabin on a little creek where he was trapping at the time. In a day and a half, we had a semblance of a cabin that was usable to keep you warm. We developed a system of making a cabin that was very quick and very efficient. It was certainly nothing to look at, but it got you in out of the cold. That was what we were mostly concerned about. I liked building cabins and have fond memories of several.

Wilson always worried about the perception and reputation of the trapping industry. He was known as the "Patriarch of Alaska Trappers," an informal title that signified the respect he's earned through hard work, integrity, and wisdom.

When I was a young kid, there were very few trapline disputes because people just didn't mess around somebody else's trapline. As the population of Alaska grew and trapping became profitable, people would move in on another person's trapline and not have respect for it. One my goals in trapping was to be an example of good ethics. In furbuying, too, I wanted to show good ethics and have respect within the industry. That was very important to me.

One of the worst things we can have in the trapping community is a bad image in the public eye. As an industry, I think we succeeded in conveying a good image. Ethics are grounded in the culture of the trapping community. I'm glad for that. I think we have to keep on getting the word out, and keep educating the new trappers that are coming into the fraternity.

{DEAN WILSON PASSED AWAY IN 2010}

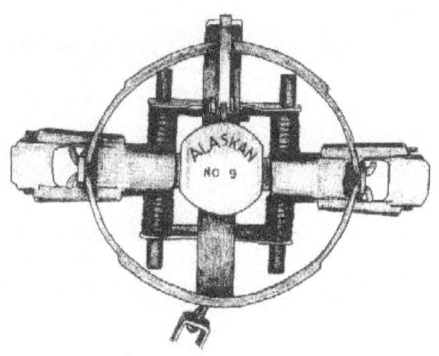

Northwest

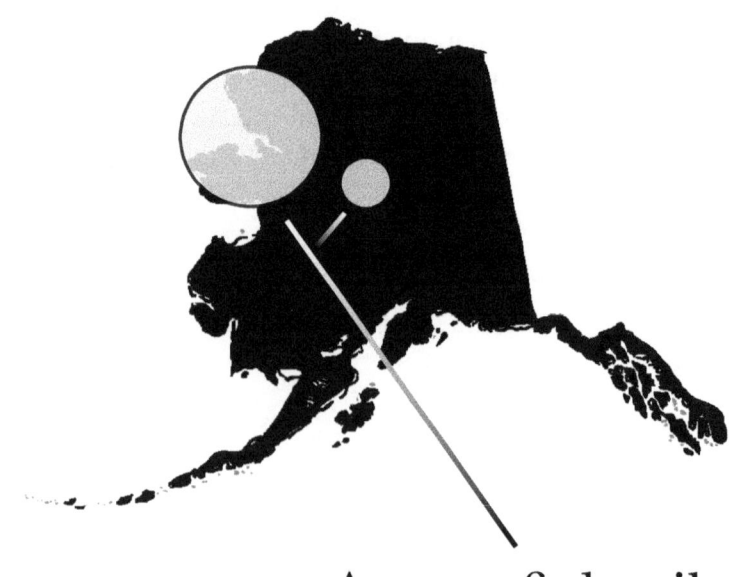

Areas of detail

BETTLES, KOTZEBUE, NOME

BILL FICKUS
Bettles, AK

Bill Fickus grew up on a farm in Pennsylvania. From a young age, he hunted and trapped, yearning for a life in the wilderness. Bill moved to Alaska as a young man and settled temporarily in the small community of North Pole. He learned to fly small airplanes, and worked as a pilot for a small air taxi operation. Bill married an Athabaskan Indian. The young couple moved their family to a gold mining claim in the Brooks Range, north of the small village of Bettles.

I came up to Alaska in 1956. I went to work as a machinist at Eielson. I used to fly The Bush years ago when Alaska was a territory. Lill and I got married in '59. She's a full Native, born in Arctic Village. I'd been wanting to get out of the Fairbanks area, so in '63 we moved up here to what we named the Crevice Creek Ranch, north of Bettles. I mined gold in the summer and trapped in the winter. We had two kids then. The idea was we were just going to stay here until the kids got school-aged and then we were going to go back to Fairbanks. Instead, we started the kids in correspondence classes and ended up home schooling all four kids. They all turned out real well. We were a close-knit family.

In about '65, I started getting interested in taking hunters out. I was not a guide. I was more of a transporter. We'd put them up here and then I'd charge them so much for flying. I passed the written test for guiding in late '66. I'd do a little mining in the summer-time, guiding in the fall, and then trapping in the winter.

A trapline in the Brooks Range is the ultimate dream for many trappers. For Bill, it was right out his back door. He welcomed both the challenge and income he derived by trapping Alaska's furbearers.

I did most of my trapping with dogs. We didn't get our first snowmachine 'til 1975. I liked dogs better. You had to feed them all summer long, but they're so much better. When I was trapping with dogs, I learned wolves liked to follow our trail. The smell of the dogs put the wolves at ease. As a result, my favorite set for wolves is a simple trail set.

I had 180 traps set out on one 'line. We'd occasionally get a big snow with lots of wind. The traps would get buried. It was hard for me to find them. Those dogs knew where every one was. They would stop at every trap. When they did that, I'd know, "I've got a trap here somewhere."

I had a 69-mile-long 'line north of here. It would take me one or two days. Halfway around the loop, I had a tent. Never had a cabin.

Our primary furs were lynx, wolf and wolverine. My best year was 35 lynx. That's when lynx were going for $600. That was a good season. My favorite set for a lynx was an open cubby. Most of the time, you can find a natural one in the willows. I'd tie a duck or grouse wing on a piece of dental floss and hang it about two feet above the snow. I'd place the trap six inches out in front. It worked on lynx, fox and wolverine.

Bill's guiding operation was low-key in the sense of self-promotion, but high-caliber in the sense of great animals and wilderness values.

All the years I guided, I never advertised. Your hunters will tell everybody if they had a good hunt. I always worked alone; never hired assistant guides. When I had the horses, my wife would hunt with me and then the kids would wrangle. The whole family would be involved.

I've always gotten along good with the game wardens. They treated me fine. Of course, I never violated so that made a big difference. I have to say, Joe Abrams was a heck of a nice guy. He was based out of Bettles. If there was a family that needed meat, and maybe unemployed, he'd look the other way.

He was also good for catching the bad guys! He had an ivory-colored Super Cub with big old tires on it. A couple guys were out on a foggy day. They figured no airplane would be flying in. The color of the plane allowed him to approach almost undetected. You'd hear the "putt putt" of the engine and first thing you'd see coming through the fog was two big tires. That was Joe Abram catching the bad guys! He'd nail them!

It's hard for me to pick a favorite animal to hunt. I love 'em all. I guess the best is the grizzly. They're a challenge. A moose is just a lot of work. Sheep would be my next one. And of course caribou. They used to be so plentiful here you just went out and shot as many as you needed and that was it. They used to come through by the hundreds of thousands. In the fall time, the hills would be crawling with caribou. The herd was estimated at 250,000. I think there were a lot more than that.

Bill had a deep and abiding respect for grizzly bears. His keen observational skills provided an intimate understanding of bear behavior. Like many an Alaskan hunter before him, Bill has had some close calls.

The most bear hunters I had in one season was three. The first year I guided, we took three bears and all of them made the [Boone and Crockett] book.

One of them scored ninth for world record. We took two moose that made the record book that same year.

One of my hunters took a shot at a grizzly. I saw the bear lurch and then he dropped down into a small creek bed. We kept looking for him. I got about 15 feet from a clump of brush. I saw the bear crouch like a cat does when it gets ready to spring. If I would have taken one more step to clear that brush, he would have had me. I had my gun ready and I called the hunter, "If you want to shoot, you better get over here right now." He came over and when he shot, I shot. It was too close to take a chance. Turned out the first shot was just a flesh wound.

A few years before that, we took a boar … a nice bear. We were coming off a sheep hunt. We spotted the bear from the top of the hill. The bear caught our scent and ran away. I thought we spooked him, so we started wading across the Allen River. Something told me to turn around and there was the bear coming out. As he leaped, I turned and shot.

You hear debates about which way the impact of a shot will cause an animal to fall. This bear was in a full charge and it was really a bad shot. Let's say it was a well-placed gut shot. The impact put him right back up on the bank. 'Course this was almost at muzzle velocity. It stopped his forward charge, and knocked him right back. He'd been fighting and was apparently in a bad mood.

A few years ago, I was coming back from mining up the creek. I was riding my three-wheeler. There is an "S" turn in the trail. Just before I made a left turn, I see a bear and a two-year-old cub maybe 90, 100 yards away. The cub was about the same size as the sow. They instantly charged. I hollered and they never slowed down. So I took the .44 and I threw a shot over their heads and then threw another shot in front of them. No effect. So I put the pedal to the metal on the three-wheeler and took off. She caught me on the right hand corner, took a swipe at me and my hat came off.

When I got back home, my wife asked me what happened.

I said, "What do you mean?"

She said, "You've got blood all over your face."

There was a claw mark right under my eye. I never even knew the bear touched me. I realized I lost my hat, but I didn't realize the bear knocked it off.

We had a bunkhouse up at our mining claim. We always had somebody spend the night up there because the bears liked to break in. A friend who was working with us, it was his turn to be up at the claim. He came back in 20 minutes saying, "She's back again." I took the .06 with me this time. Sure enough, we get about 100 yards away and she starts walking toward us. We moved to the side. She just changed her compass heading and she started running towards us. When she got about 30 feet away, I said, "She drew blood on me two days ago. That's close enough." So we busted her.

Bill also hunted Dall sheep. Those hunts were often arduous and frustrating, but Bill is very proud all his sheep hunts were 100-percent successful for the hunters.

My favorite sheep hunt was any hunt we did with the horses, 'cause I did enough packing before we got 'em. Once those horses learn where you're going, it's even easier. After you go a half a mile, they'll know where you're heading. You can just take a loose dally on the reins and sit back and shoot the breeze. The way we did it, a hunt for sheep on horses takes three days. One day to get into the mountains, one day on the hunt and then one day back. If you score, you might spend an extra day in camp and come back on the fourth day. I usually booked the clients for seven days. That way, if you get rained out or wolves chase our sheep off, we've still got time to figure out another option. You come back in, resupply, and go back out somewhere else. I've never had one hunter go home skunked.

One year, we had two sheep hunters, Vernon and Grover. We were about 75 yards away from the sheep. Vernon took the first shot. He had a one-shot kill. If you don't move, the other sheep will bolt for a short distance but then they'll stop. Grover should have known better, but he started shooting as soon as they bolted. He missed on a running shot. This one big ram stopped about 250 to 300 yards away. He nailed it and the ram went down. We're shaking hands and congratulating each other. Lill looks up and says, "Hey your sheep is getting away."

We went miles hunting for that sheep. It wasn't leaving hardly any blood. We decided to go back and get the plane to help find him. We eventually spotted him. He was right at the mouth of a cave. When the weather goes bad, the sheep hide in there. After the hunters left, I wanted to find that sheep. We went up into that cave to look for that sheep but it was gone. When I was out with the next hunter, we spotted that ram! He was feeding with about six other rams. It was two weeks later and he was still doing fine, at least until we shot him. When he skinned him out, the wound from Grover's shot was already healed. That original shot entered an inch from the center-line on top of his head. He must have turned his head enough where it went in and came out with minimal damage.

The most sheep I ever took out of our area was six. Usually, I'd rather only take out four. That way you take your best rams out and you don't over hunt.

When we were hunting sheep, we got into some pretty steep places. There's one ridge with a good foot path. It's about 18 to 24 inches wide. But it's almost a sheer drop down on either side; about ten degrees from vertical. I had a hunter up there one time that panicked. He got part way across and then wouldn't go either way. He froze. I had to pack his rifle across while he crawled. He finally got a sheep on Bar Creek. After he shot that sheep, it slid down the mountain and landed in a big hole. We lowered Lill down on a rope. We pulled the sheep up first and then later tossed the rope back down and pulled her up.

Moose and caribou were highly desired by Bill's clients. The Brooks Range is home to both species. All hunts generate stories and foibles, and Bill has no problem laughing at his mistakes.

We had a guy up on his first hunt. I landed on a bar down river and we went in on a lake. A moose was bedded down in these big tall trees, making it hard to find. We walked up within 20 feet of that moose. It was sound asleep! The hunter shoots and misses the moose. I mean, point blank range almost! Misses! So he shoots again and he wounds it. The moose gets up and runs into the lake, into about four to five inches of water. He shot five or six times. I had to go back to the plane to get more ammo for him. It took me maybe 30 minutes to go back and forth. I went out in the lake and kept spraying bullets right in front of the moose's nose with the ought-six to get him back to the shoreline. When he reached solid ground, the hunter busted him. We had another guy on a moose hunt. We spotted a moose swimming to the far side of the lake. He wanted that moose real bad. I said, "Okay, but don't shoot him in the water." The moose gets about ten feet from the water and I said, "Okay, you can shoot him now." We're shooting a good 250 yards across the lake. He gets the perfect heart-lung shot. What happens? The moose backpedals, goes over backwards, and lands right in the lake. I had to go back to the airplane, get a rope, lasso him and pull him in.

We had a guy out on a caribou hunt. We went to an area where there were bands of anywhere from 50 to 3,500 caribou. They were all migrating south. I said, "We'll just land on the bar ahead of them and let them walk up on us." It took us three or four gravel-bar landings before we got one. That's usually how it works! After a whole day of trying to get one caribou, we came back here to the Ranch and there must have been 1,500 to 2,000 caribou bedded down outside the fence of my horse pasture! Apparently, they just didn't understand the fence. They'd come up to it, get poked, and just lay down.

Like many Alaskans, Bill did a little bit of everything to feed his family and thrive in the wilderness. He was proud of his accomplishments. He was a contented man who would " ... do it all over again."

When we moved up here, we realized it was something which we should have done earlier. If I had it to do over again, I would make a few changes, but not very much. It was a good life for the kids. They grew up free of drugs and all of them are smart. They've all got good jobs now and they've all got families of their own. They are all hunters and three of my four kids are licensed pilots. It's been a good life. I was never rich, but then we never went hungry.

{BILL FICKUS PASSED AWAY IN 2007}

BOB UHL
Kotzebue, AK

Bob Uhl grew up in California during the 1930s and '40s. He was drafted into military service near the end of World War II. Bob served in a platoon commonly known as the "Alaska Scouts." The group was composed of hunters, trappers and Alaska Natives.

I f you would enlist for a regular hitch of three years, they would give you choice of theater and branch of service. I had been outdoor-oriented most of my young life and I always wanted to go to Alaska.

It turned out there was no other infantry outfit in Alaska except the remnants of the Alaska Scouts. Another name for the outfit was "Castner's Cut-Throats." They were made up of trappers, Eskimos, and outdoor people from all over the state.

Here I was, 19 years old with a whole bunch of people that had really operated outdoors in Alaska. It turned out to be great for me. That particular outfit was still making extended trips. One of our summer trips was to boat up the river from Bethel and do some mapping of the Portage area where the Yukon and Kuskokwim come together. All that experience helped shape my later life of living off the land.

After the end of the War, our platoon was broken up. The Air Corps wanted us to provide arctic survival training for all their flying officer personnel. In the winter of '48, we established an Arctic indoctrination school in Kotzebue.

While stationed in Kotzebue, Bob had extensive exposure to the indigenous culture. He met and married an Eskimo woman. He credits his wife's family with teaching him to live a subsistence lifestyle.

I was a pretty impressionable young man in 1948. Remember the timing. Hiroshima had just been bombed a couple years earlier. To some of us in that era, things didn't look all that great on the world scene. I had the good fortune of coming in contact with a group of people ... living off the land.

During that time in Kotzebue I met Carrie, who was Eskimo. We were married in May '48. We now live northwest of Kotzebue. The Eskimo name of this location is "Place of White Whales." This is their summer camp where they came for fishing.

What impressed me was their almost complete independence of money. Being young and fairly tough, I needed to find out how they managed to do it. I had good teachers.

Carrie's dad was one of those teachers. He and I got scolded one time. He lived with missionaries for some time and he was quite proud of his ability to speak English. Of course I couldn't speak Eskimo and I was full of questions. Every time I'd ask a question, he would answer in English to me and be proud of that. Carrie's mother broke in one day and said, "You're making a mistake there, old man. You should respond to him in Eskimo and he would soon learn to talk Eskimo." She was right. I have gone these many years and I still can't carry on a conversation in Eskimo. Of course I recognize phrases and words and names of everything all right, but I'm still not fluent in Eskimo and she pin-pointed the reason right there.

Bob learned hunting methods from his in-laws. His family's diet consisted of fish, game, plants, birds, and marine mammals gathered in the area. Knowledge of the animals was vital.

People here are oriented toward bearded seals. That's opposed to those at Point Hope that are bowhead whale-oriented, or some of the southern villages are walrus-oriented. The situation is similar. The products are pretty much all the same. Each of those species has something you can use for clothing and something you can eat. It is just a different marine mammal species that has been the mainstay of the people through the many years.

To hunt bearded seals, you enter a different world. It is a world of ice, an ocean of ice. You start harvesting in the latter part of April, and then you spend the next two months out on the ice 'most every day, day and night. You spend a lot of time up on the higher points, ice bergs, scanning with binoculars looking for seals laying on the ice.

I soon learned the Eskimo people don't have much sympathy for letting one get away. By being cautious, you're supposed to get close enough so there is no danger of losing the animal and that means a neck shot. Even with the high cost of ammunition and the lack of money, it was common practice to shoot each animal twice. That was kind of a sign of success if you hear somebody shoot twice — BOOM — BOOM.

The bearded seal is the prize everybody wants. That of course is what the whole culture used to walk on. There was no other leather. Bearded seals provided the mukluk and moccasin soles for everybody. The blubber, of course, turns to seal oil.

At that time, the main source of local income was the seal oil business. After hunting for two to three months, you would have more seal oil than you'd need yourself. The oil is stored in seal pokes and they can be traded for fairly large money. They are traded to the Indians from the Kobuk River region. You never had any trouble selling your seal oil and that was where your monetary income came from.

Local furbearers provided furs for garments, as well as additional income via the fur market.

The one other local source of money in the region was from furs. So you quite naturally become a fur hunter. Carrie's brothers were herders during the reindeer era, but the reindeer were disappearing. They found a pretty good income from hunting foxes, both white and red. The method of catching foxes back then had nothing to do with traps. For the most part everybody realized a fox makes a track, and at the end of that track there's a fox. So they put on snowshoes or skis and they'd just walk them down.

One of the big things about trapping is it gives you a reason to be outdoors and amongst the animals. That allows you to learn a whole lot about them you really didn't expect. And you need to learn those things, particularly if you're depending on that animal for income.

In that era, stuff like flour and sugar was very cheap at the local stores. One red fox might get you $150 to $200 and for that you could get a whole sled load of stuff from the store.

Caribou are another key player in the ecosystem of Northwest Alaska.

Caribou are one of the most choice animals of the region. When they're around everybody is happy because you have a reliable supply of good meat. Eskimo people depended on caribou herds because they supply so much of your basic needs. If you add caribou to the fish and marine animals that are here, your life becomes much easier. In addition to the meat, caribou provided furs for making cold-weather clothes. A caribou is a very wonderful animal and their population was building all through this period that I have been here.

For us, you can't separate caribou hunting from trapping activity, because if you're up there caribou hunting you always take a dozen traps along for foxes.

Beluga whales were another important component of the Eskimo lifestyle. Bob has noticed a change in the population.

The ideal way to catch belugas is when they are in shallow water. Here in Kotzebue Sound, you have shallow water but normally the beluga don't go in the shallow water of their own accord. The strategy was to anchor boats between here and Kotzebue, on the edge of shallow water. We kept everything silent, just waiting for these huge groups of sometimes 100, 200 beluga to work their way in. When they get past where your boats are anchored, then everybody worked together and drove them farther into shallow water. Nobody had any engines, so we just worked together to drive them with kayaks and skin boats.

Then, the first engine boats began to show up. So the kayaks and the skin boats and those engine boats would drive them into shallow water and kill them. Gradually, the old system of working together to drive the belugas broke up. With engine boats, people could more easily pursue individual belugas or small groups. It became 'every boat for itself.' One almost sure way to catch a beluga would be to search for a female with a newborn calf, because the female has to wait for the calf to come up and it is relatively easy to keep track of a female with a newborn calf. The drying racks would be just white with beluga muktuk hanging.

2003 is the first year since 1948 that nobody has seen a beluga through the whole period of the time beluga are supposed to be in Kotzebue Sound.

My theory is that with the change of hunting methods, it was so easy to catch newborn calves with females we have eliminated that portion of the population in Kotzebue Sound with innate homing instinct. There's no problem with the overall beluga stock, but at the same time they are avoiding Kotzebue Sound.

Alaska is known for its wild weather, and the area near Kotzebue has some of the wildest.

You're pretty much at the mercy of the weather in this country. Long spells of bad weather could cause you to run out of dog feed. Of course the people depended on the dogs. You had to have a dog team in order to go caribou hunting or trapping, and you needed to keep the dogs fed.

We don't have much elevation from the ocean here and we have had two recent storms that threatened our homes. The worst one we have seen was when the storm came in from the south, from the mouth of the Sound. You look out there and see the tops of the huge swells and they seem way above the level of our homes. Then at the same time, the water level in the lagoon behind us began to rise. So, with the waves coming higher from the front and the lagoon getting higher from the back, the living area here gets narrower and narrower. Those storms are a little frightening. We don't have much room for the levels to rise much. We had to move out.

Whales and caribou aren't the only wildlife providing sustenance for local people. The residents of Northwest Alaska have a varied diet.

We probably live as much off birds as we do off of marine mammal oil and meat. This is great waterfowl country. Northern pintail is our "bread and butter" duck here. Waterfowl is a big part of our diet, but fish is the biggest thing. Everybody talks about marine mammals and of course the big game animals, but for the most part the people of the whole region around here are dependent more on fish than anything else as far as diet goes. One thing you never quite realize until you're into it is what living off the land really amounts to. You've got to come up with something to eat almost every day in order to have a varied and pleasing diet.

From the beginning, Bob knew his only chance for success was to learn from those who had come before him. He is grateful to those who shared their knowledge and skills, giving him a chance to thrive in the Great Land.

My life here in the Sound has meant everything to me. The first eye-opener came when I entered Alaska right into the arms of this bunch of trappers and Eskimos and Alaska outdoorsmen while in the Army. That just made me want to learn more about it, enough of it so I could live that way, too. For me it has been a special privilege to live that close to nature, to the animals, to the land. I'm very thankful for that and appreciate the people that were willing to act as my teachers.

DANIEL KARMUN

Nome, AK

Daniel Karmun was born and raised in the village of Deering on the North side of the Seward Peninsula. His Inupiat ancestors arrived in Alaska from Russia. The Inupiat have lived a subsistence lifestyle in the harsh regions of the north for generations. Daniel's family subscribed to this lifestyle, changing activities and food as the seasons did. Daniel uses the annual cycle of hunting, fishing, and gathering to portray the wide variety of activities necessary for his people to survive. Each spring began with seal hunting, the most important element of the Inupiat diet.

My Eskimo name is Kakashinonuk. I'm named after my late uncle who was a dog teamer way back in the 1930s. My grandfather and grandmother originally migrated from Siberia in the early 1900s. My papa came from over there and married my mother in Deering.

The spring season is when a lot of Inupiat people are making preparations for hunting on the ice. We first hunt for the seals that stay on top of the ice when the sun comes out. In addition to the meat, we use the seal hides to make seal pokes. Back in the 1930s, there were no buckets or other containers like we have today. They would take the meat and blubber off the seal and then turn the skin inside out and fill it up with air. After drying for about a week, those will be our containers for the coming summer season. We always need containers like the seal poke to store our food sources, like the marine mammals from the ocean in the spring-time or berries in the fall-time.

We would go seal hunting as long as the winds weren't blowing from the east. When the wind blows from the east, you can hear for great long distance and the seals will hear us, too. So we'd go out when the winds are opposite the east wind. You can get pretty close to a seal (within 25 yards) just crawling with good seal skin pants and mukluks on. You make sure the seal doesn't hear you. We always try to have a little barrier that will hide you as you crawl on the ice. You don't do it in a rush.

After the seal hunting, the men bring the seals home. The women start cutting up seals so they can dry. Spring is a good season where the sun stays out for a long time. During June, the sun does not set. That's when we dry up a lot of the food for the winter.

If we found a floating walrus, we'd use the bottom of the walrus. We wouldn't use the top, because the sun had already spoiled it. But a walrus is so big and the water is so cold you could use the bottom.

As spring progressed, they harvested bearded seals for meat and oil.

The ice breaks around end of May. That's when we'd go hunting for bearded seal on the ice floes out in the ocean. When the sun is shining, that's when they stay on top of the ice. You've got to select your days to hunt out in the ocean and make sure the weather is good. Upon catching our bearded seal, we'd split open the belly and take all the innards out.

They weigh about 1,000 pounds. That's where we get the blubber we render into oil. After cleaning out the innards we'd put that bearded seal back into water, tie it up, and wash it up. We were always taking those precautions to make sure the food won't spoil on us.

When we got a boat load of bearded seal, then we'd head home. You can handle about half a dozen. Back at the village, we'd divide the catch. We'd always have a crew of four. The person that had the boat and the motor would get one extra share. We'd bring them to our families and the women folks take over the task of cutting it up. It has to be done in a certain way. Then we'd hang it up and it dries. Bearded seal meat is a delicacy for our people.

When the meat is hung up, then they'd start working on the hide and blubber. They'd spread out the skin and let the sun dry the top, so you can have a good grasp when you're cutting the blubber. If you don't dry the hide first, then it is real slippery. It is a lot of work, but they do it. We use the dried hide for our mukluk bottoms. The seal skin was also cut into long thin strips and braided to make twine that was used to tie stanchions on your sled.

The women cut the blubber and put it in a container. We render it in a place where it is cool and out of the sun. We always wanted to have plenty of oil on hand during the winter for our dry meat and dry fish. A lot of the people in the community dig underground storage areas to keep their products frozen. They're about ten feet by six feet.

As the migratory birds returned, the Eskimos welcomed the new source of fresh meat. They collected "greens" in early summer, adding nutrients and flavor to the diet.

After seal hunting at the end of May, the geese, the cranes, and all the birds start migrating northwest. There are areas where they nest every year. We'll go to several locations where there are a lot of lakes. If the river beach sand is visible, they'll land there, too. They get their feed from the grass. We'll get an abundance of birds and other food to last us the whole winter.

We hunt them every spring.

Them days we'd get eggs from the geese, cranes, whatever. My papa took us out camping where the seagulls nested on a bluff. My older brother would climb down the bluff, and someone would watch the rope on top. He'd use the rope to go down to get the eggs. He would fill his shirt front and back. When it was full he'd tug on the line to let the guy know to secure the line, making sure he can come up safely. We'd freeze the eggs for winter use.

Right after spring break-up, we'd pick what we called the "greens."

They grow on willows. We'd also have what we called the sweet potato. We trapped squirrels in the springtime to make jackets.

We never had stove oil. We could get coal from a mine about 50 miles southeast of us. We'd get a few 100 pound sacks for the winter. If we had any extra, we would sell a bag for one dollar. We'd mix the coal with wood.

Fishing season in the summer brought another source of fresh protein. Fishing was a major activity. It involved not only catching the fish, but also processing them. The whole family was involved.

Then the fishing season comes on us. During the winter, the older folks taught us how to make fish nets. When the ice is breaking up the whitefish and the trout come. We catch them with a seine, cut them up, and dry them. That is an activity you repeat every year.

If we made a big catch with the seine, we might have too many fish to cut at once. We'd dig holes and throw the fish in the hole for dog food. The meat ages during the course of the summer and that is what the dogs like.

Years ago, dogs were the only source of transportation we had for hunting, trapping, and reindeer herding. There were a lot of dogs in the village. We fed them salmon, humpies mostly. When we're cutting the salmon for dog food, we'll leave the head on. That makes it recognizable as dog feed. If a fish is intended for human consumption, we'll cut the head off.

The ripe berries of late summer required lots of work, but offered a sweet treat and added important nutrients to the winter diet.

After the fishing season is over, the berry season occurs. Normally, the blueberries ripen around the first of August. Then the salmonberries are next, about the middle of August. We sometime have to go greater distances to pick those. Then the blackberries, around September 1. Then the cranberries just before freeze up. Those are the four groups of berries that we have up here. The berries were stored in the seal pokes that I described earlier.

I've never witnessed a lack of berries. They're always there. The other food items we depend on – the roots, the greens, the seal oil is always there. With the changing climate, you don't know what it is going to happen in the future.

Early autumn was a time to pursue ptarmigan, hares, and some late season fish.

During the fall season, we were always going after rabbits and ptarmigans. We'd also go up the Niukluk River to spear some fish during the night. We'd use a one-mantle lantern with a little shade and look for trout and whitefish in the water. It was fun. A lot of the fish we catch in the fall we'd eat it frozen.

Trapping season in early winter provided furs for garments and also offered one of the few sources of cash.

Towards fall when the snow comes and things freeze up, the men folks go out to the country to do a lot of trapping and hunting. They used mostly foot-hold traps. They'd trap for any types of furs they can find – red fox, white fox, cross fox; on occasion, they'll get wolverines and wolves. That's the five types of furs they can depend on. Fur prices were good them days back in the 1920s and '30s.

Some of the young people and elderly ladies in the community will go out and set little snares for ptarmigans and rabbits. It was always a good time for our men folks just before Christmas. We'd come home with the furs and buy gifts.

Reindeer herding in late winter gave the community fresh meat at a time when it was otherwise scarce, as well as another source of fur for garments.

The family went to the reindeer operation right after New Years. They'd pull their kids out of school and go reindeer herding. Working the reindeer generated meat products, skin products, sinew, and leggings that can be used for making mukluks and parkees. It starts in January and lasts for two months. There was hardly any thought about keeping your kids in school.

There are a lot of bears around during reindeer-fawning season. The herders sometimes kill bears when they come after the fawns. We had the privilege of protecting that resource.

They first brought reindeer over from Siberia in 1891. The late Dr. Sheldon Jackson brought ten live deer. The reason they brought over deer was because the whalers came up every spring to hunt whales and they were depleting that resource. Inupiat people had always depended on the whales for food. So they tried to bring in another animal that can provide meat like the reindeer. From that ten head of reindeer that were brought over, about 30 years later it increased to about 300,000. Certain members of the community were in charge of the reindeer. My papa was in charge of the herd at Deering.

Teaching skills to the next generation has always been important in the Inupiat culture.

When a boy turned 13, he was expected to behave more like an adult. I remember so well my parents telling my older brothers to include me on a seal hunting trip. We went with the dog team down to Cape Espenberg where we hunted seal. That was my first time I went out. That was the custom of the other families, as well. Of course, the woman folks taught their daughters important lessons after they turned 13 years old, too.

I got my first seal on that trip. Papa and mama said, "You give your first catch to an elder in the community." That was the custom of our culture. I never forgot what that elderly lady said (in Eskimo), "God bless you with many more things." That lived with me all my life. I never forget that.

My wife worked in the school for 21 years. Her co-workers were always asking her, "How does your husband get moose every time he goes out?" I finally told her we had an elder blessing years ago and it still lives.

My wife and I only went up to eighth grade, but we had the greatest instructors in our parents and the elders in our community. We were taught to take care of every person in the community whether they're young or old, especially doing things to satisfy the elders. That's still vital for our people.

Our granddaughter is married now and has kids. About two years ago, their kids wanted to learn how to cut fish. So we went down to our camp and set out a seine. Our parents taught us our chores to bring fish to the cutting board. It is a custom we were trying to keep alive. My wife and I had a lot of fun.

Our grandson now does the hunting for us out in the ocean. It is getting too hard for me to do any more. We still do a lot of fishing, cutting fish, trying to teach our children, grandchildren, and great-grandchildren. We teach them how to pick berries and dry fish. We try to pass on the customs of our Inupiat culture. It is hard to do in this modern day and age we live in.

Central and Western Interior

Area of detail

Fairbanks, McGrath, Nabesna, Minto

RICHARD FRANK
Fairbanks, AK

Richard Frank grew up in the village of Minto, west of Fairbanks. He spent considerable time in fishing camps on the Yukon River and trapping camps north of the Yukon. As a young boy, he lived the traditional subsistence lifestyle of his Athabaskan heritage.

When I was young, we lived on the Wood River off of the Yukon River. Trapping in that area was mostly for marten. There were a few wolves and lynx, but not too many mink. When we lived in Minto, it was mostly mink and muskrats.

My dad was quite a trapper, as were my brothers. They would leave after freeze-up. They'd go trapping up in the Kanuti country. They lived in tents. They also "camped out" by making a shelter under a tree. We wouldn't see dad or the older boys until after New Years. Boy, did they bring back a load of fur. In my young days, I realized trapping was really important for the family. I always maintain that trappers are the ones that kept the economy going.

My mother and us younger kids would stay behind. There were no radios and nobody around. I thought we were lucky to be so isolated. A guy from Rampart came by to check on us, just to see how we were doing. That's the way it was back then. People had an honor system of checking on each other.

In the old days, there were some good times and there were some times that was pretty hard. The old people used to share some of their experience with us by telling us stories. In that way, they taught us what to do and what not to do.

Traps were in limited supply in the Rampart store. When they were out … they were out. We'd go to Nenana and they'd be out also. We used to take snares apart to make two snares out of one. You had to make do with what you had.

In 1950, I landed on the Chena River with a bush pilot. I had a sack of fur and went to NC Company. They had groceries, hardware, ammunition, traps, everything I needed. I took my fur there and they gave me $200. That's a lot of money in those days. Come in the big city right from the trapline where you live in a tent. Come into the city and throw fur on the table and get money back. That was real life.

A subsistence lifestyle is year-round. You're either finding food, preparing food, preserving food or storing food.

We had gardens in the village and gardens at the fish camp. My job was to keep them watered and hoed down. We had a root cellar in Minto where we stored our vegetables. At fish camp, we stored fish, moose, and vegetables in a root cellar. We covered it and put logs up on top. Next winter, we had fresh fish and fresh meat. That was part of life.

Almost everything in a fish wheel was homemade. The only things we bought were the wire and nails. It took 60 poles for each fish wheel. The Old Man wasn't satisfied with one wheel. He had about three or four of them. That was a lot of work to build, but was also a big supply of food. We moved the fish wheel downstream by paddling. To pull it upstream, he'd build what they call a Spanish windlass. He made the system work. We got fish.

In the Bush, log cabins are the residence of choice and necessity.

My brother Alfred had a cabin on Birch Creek. A weasel used to come through the ventilator and run around the cabin. I asked him, "Why don't you trap it?" He reminded me it was a sign of good luck. That's an old Indian way. You don't kill everything. He was trying to share the good life with other animals. That was what we were taught also.

That cabin had history written on the walls:

"September 23, 1939 one bull moose."
"December 1938 so many marten and mink."

It was sort of like a museum. I used to go there to see that writing on the wall. All that history was lost when the cabin burned up.

Muskrats provide a source of income for enterprising hunters.

One year, muskrats were selling for 60 cents apiece and it was common for people to take 1,000 muskrats. There were so many muskrats, people from Tanana, Stevens Village, Rampart, Nenana, and even McGrath would come into Minto Flats for the annual spring hunt. It was common to see one carton of .22 shells for each muskrat hunter. That's a lot of ammunition, but there was a lot of muskrats. At 60 cents per pelt, if you get 1,000, that's $600. That's a lot of money in those days. It bought a lot of things: gas for the summer, food supply for the winter.

Richard learned about wolves both from elders' stories and his own experiences.

My father used to tell us about hunting wolves. If you get surrounded by wolves when you're on snowshoes, put the snowshoes on your back side and hold a willow and your rifle in front of you. They won't come up to you then. I don't know if I could stay that cool, but that was the way it was done. There were two young boys that had done it. They were surrounded by a whole bunch of wolves and they kept their cool. The elders didn't believe it, but they went out and saw the tracks and confirmed it.

########

I was on the trapline in 1952, when I heard a commotion. I saw a moose running. He came crashing through the brush with five wolves behind him. Two of the wolves split up, one on each side of the moose, just to guide it. The moose stopped and that's where they got him. One wolf in back came up and caught the moose by the neck. That was quite an experience seeing those wolves take down a big moose like that.

My brother Alfred used to take wolf pups out of the dens. He is the last person I know who did that. There are a lot of wolves in Minto Flats. There are too many wolves out there doing a lot of damage to other animals. I think we have to exercise more different avenues in making the balance work. Not everybody is going to be satisfied.

I always maintain that trappers are the ones that keep wolves under control and help to maintain the balance of nature. The most I've seen in one bunch in the Minto Flats was 22. That's a pretty big bunch. One time, a friend flew me around on the Flats. We counted 16 moose kills. The wolves hadn't even eaten them up. The moose were just killed and left.

I've participated in the aerial wolf hunt. Bill Carlo was the pilot. He told me the same thing as my dad taught me. We were taught the young wolves are at the front of a running pack and they take turns. When you see a bunch of wolves together, don't shoot the one in front. Get the ones in the middle. If you get the leader, the others will just mill around. We made two passes with the plane and I got two wolves. Dad and Bill were right … the other wolves just milled around. We landed the airplane they didn't run away. They were sticking around for the leaders.

Snowshoes were built from local trees. It was a long and detailed process, but crucial for winter transportation.

We use birch to make our snowshoes. Some people have the knack of selecting the best trees. They check to see if it is straight, no knots. Some guys would take a little chip off the tree and put it in their mouth to see if it bent properly.

One guy knew I was going to look for birch. He said, "I want you to come with me." We spent all day. He cut some trees and split them. We came back to the village that night. He said, "We'll go back down there tomorrow to get the wood." He used those trees to build a little trapline sled. He also built snowshoes and spoons and lots of other things. His name was Jimmy Bruce.

The next year, we had to haul some gear out to camp for these old people. Jimmy came out and told me to use his sled. That's the sled he built when we were looking for birch. So the cycle kept on growing of helping each other.

I'm named after a part of a snowshoe. The cross piece in front on your foot is called the Shintift. Shintift is my Indian name. Those names had a lot to do with how we identify ourselves. When I introduce myself to other old people, I introduce myself as Shintift, Tochute Tribe. Tochute is a fish tribe. When the older people hear that, they know who is my family and where I came from.

Interior villages relied heavily on caribou and moose for meat.

Caribou would come over the hill, headed for the Yukon River. Caribou would be milling all over. My father made us kids stay in the smokehouse to keep from getting trampled. The dogs would be trying to jerk free to get the caribou. As a young fellow, I thought there would never be an end to it. We waited for a certain time of the year when their meat is really good. That's when we went to get some animals.

When the caribou were so abundant, there were very few moose in Minto Flats. One time, the old people and the young men were having tea together. A young trapper came in and said there was a moose track across the trail. One old fellow got up and spoke. He called three young men in their Native name. He said, "Tomorrow morning you're going to go check on that moose." As soon as he sat down, they went out. They were challenged right there in front of everybody to go check on the moose. They went to bed early so they could hunt the next day. They got it.

Dog teams provided the best transportation between villages and out to trapping cabins. Frank began mushing dogs as a young man. He quickly mastered the skills and earned a reputation as an excellent musher.

They had a bunch of dogs at St. Mark's Mission in Nenana. They were closing up the mission so the priest asked me if I wanted to take over the dogs. I ended up with seven dogs. They weren't really trained. That's how I got started mushing dogs.

After I got a dog team, it was pretty neat, but being on foot was better. You get to appreciate the land and animals and the birds when you're walking. Whereas, when you're on a dog team, you're watching dogs and watching the trail. You only have time to take a glance here and there. One old fellow told me, "Don't just rush through the land from one place to another. You don't appreciate what we have with your heart. You've got to stop and have a cup of tea." He was right. I'll never forget that. There were so many things they taught us.

One spring, the boys at Minto said, "Let's put our dogs together and send someone to Anchorage for the dog races." They selected me as the driver. I took 14 dogs. This was my very first major race. I came in third. The dogs were prepared, but not the musher. I was inexperienced. The guys that had the experience should have raced that team.

A couple years later, Gareth Wright called up and said, "I want you to help me train dogs." The North American was coming up. Three days before the race he said, "You're going to mush the dogs." I told him, "Like hell I am. That's your team." He was going to have an operation so that's how I got in the North American. I damn near won it.

As a teenager, Richard had a disagreement with his parents regarding the value of a formal education. The harsh lesson he learned that day led to a varied working life.

When I was 13 years old, I told my mother and father I was going to quit school and go trapping like my other friends. My Father jumped up and grabbed me and took me to the door. He told me, "If you're sick or you want to go back to school, you can come back. Otherwise, you're on your own." I didn't go back. I walked from Minto to Nenana, 32 miles by trail. I left when it was dark. When I got to Nenana it was dark. On the way, I cried quite a number of times.

I went to work on the railroad in Nenana during the summer when I was 14. They told me to say I was 18. In the latter part of August, I went to work on steamer Nenana. I liked it on the riverboats. I worked my way up the ladder.

I took flying lessons at Nenana. I wanted to fly trappers in and out of their camps, 'cause fur was in abundance and most of the guys were loose with their money.

I started Minto General Store in Old Minto. It didn't work. By that time, everybody came to Fairbanks for shopping. So I bought a 15-passenger van. I named it Rock Island Bus Line after the lake I trapped on. I was after the mail contract, Minto-Livengood-Manley. The bus was doing really good until the elders got their own van. They ran me out of business.

I bid on two generators in a State surplus sale. I put $10 on one and $15 on the other. I got a letter from Juneau that said to remove the engines off their premises. I built a small shed, and put the generator in there. We cranked it up and had electric lights. An industrial company in Fairbanks had a bunch of power lines they were throwing away. They gave them to me for free. I strung a line through the brush to my mother's house and gave her electric lights ... one 50-watt light bulb. A neighbor came around and said here's $10 if you run a line to my house. I eventually bought a license. I called it Minto Power and Light. I tried a little of everything.

Frank is proud of his outdoor skills and self-sufficiency. He learned those skills and values as a boy and has passed them along to his children.

On several occasions, I've traveled to New York and Washington, DC. Coming back from New York to Alaska, a lady sat by me on the plane. She asked where I'm from and I told her Alaska. She couldn't get over that. I decided to have a little fun with her.

She asked, "How can people live in Alaska?"

I said, "How can people live in New York?"

She asked, "What do you do for a living?"

I told her, "I'm a trapper. Do you use fur? That's coming from us. Otherwise you wouldn't have fur."

She asked, "How can you live in Alaska, where you don't have any modern conveniences?"

I replied, "We don't need any."

"Savages," she said.

I said, "Who, me? Okay, let's talk about savages. The other day in New York I saw a person laying on the ground. Other people just stepped over this person. In Alaska, we don't do that. We would stop to help. Now, who's the savage?"

There's a lot of people who think of us like that.

# # # # # # # #

There was no welfare in the old days. When I was a boy, some government people came to Minto. They wanted to give welfare to my grandmother. I think it was 12 bucks a month. My dad told them, "No, we'll take care of her. If she gets welfare, she will become sick because she didn't earn it and she'd feel guilty." He convinced those people we don't need it. Those are values I share with my children. The system that we used was very honorable; otherwise the system would collapse. We worked hard and earned everything we got. It was hard but still a good life.

{RICHARD FRANK PASSED AWAY IN 2012}

SUSIE CHARLIE
Minto, AK

Susie Charlie's mom died when Susie was five years old. She was adopted and raised up by her "Auntie" and her husband in a small Tanana River village. The small family lived a meager existence. They hunted and fished for food, and trapped and cut firewood for cash income.

We lived in the village of Old Minto. My uncle died when I was 14 years old. I started to work pretty young. That's how I learned to start doing things. I used to help my Auntie cut wood. The little money we got, we used to buy our groceries ... stuff like flour, sugar, tea. We'd be lucky if we had a can of vegetable soup or a can of beans at that time. We didn't have no fancy stuff like today.

Then one of the men in the village got a contract for cutting 1,000 cords of wood for steamboats. They divided up that contract between seven camps. They felt sorry for my Auntie and gave her part of the contract. She and I cut wood all winter. We were about ten miles out of the village.

It was an every-day thing. We earned $4 a cord. It seems cheap now, but at the time it was something to us. There were no wages. Nobody had jobs. It was hard.

While we were cutting wood, we set traps for mink and muskrat. If we sell mink skin, it would be $10. If you get $35, it was lots. We had three dogs, which I used to check the traps. The dogs were smart, too. They stopped at every 'rat house, and they knew where the next mink trap is, too. They waited for us when we stopped. They knew when we got mink in the trap.

I was a little scared of both muskrat and mink. My other Auntie, her name was Sarah, a muskrat bit her thumb and wouldn't let go. She squeezed it around the neck so hard she choked it and it let her go. They didn't have medicines like today. She got some spruce pitch, warmed it up by the camp fire and put it on the wound. That's all it took.

One time, we had no traps. We made snares out of raw moose hide. We set the snares where we saw mink go in and out of a hole. My Auntie told me to try it like that. She said, "You've got to make the loop small, because the mink will slide right through." We caught two mink with those rawhide snares. I learned something there, too.

We ate the rabbits and muskrats. Muskrat was really good food. We also ate a lot of fish. My Auntie made fishtraps. She'd fix it so the fish could go inside and they can't come back out. I watched her. Everything she would do, I'd do it with her. When we'd catch enough fish, we put them in a snow hole so they would freeze. We'd leave them overnight and we'd pick them up the next day. We use the fish for our dogs, too.

My brother Teddy taught me about animals. He'd tell me how moose make noise when it walks in the water. If something howls, it would be wolf. Coyotes and fox make different noises. One time when we were camped, we heard a bunch of wolves. They tried to surround us. My brother told me, "When you camp out, you always put big rotten stump of wood in fire and it will burn all night. It keeps animals away." The elders told us wolves are scared of snowshoes. If you leave snowshoes up they wouldn't bother our camp.

Susie married in her late teens. She and her new husband (who she refers to as "Old Man") moved out into the woods. They didn't know much about living off the land.

With good advice and hard work, they accumulated the knowledge necessary to survive. They spent most of their time in pursuit of fur, fish or game.

Everybody in the village trapped in the winter. There were camps all the way out towards Murphy Dome. We saw lots of mink tracks. We set traps and checked them two times a day. Nothing. We were running out of food, so we went down to the village. We just happened to go by our trap and there was a live mink. My Old Man clubbed it and sold that mink just the way it was; didn't skin it or nothing. We got $20. It was lots to us. We buy all our groceries and went back out. We learned there weren't a lot of animals in that area. We should have looked around for fresher sign, but we didn't. We just didn't know any better.

########

One time when I went out with my Old Man, I told him, "Listen. I hear something." We waited and we saw seven lynx all come out at the same time. They were chasing rabbits. The lynx call and answer each other. Pretty soon there was a "whoosh." That was when they chased the rabbits. Some of the lynx chase and others hide so they catch the rabbits.

########

One time, we were hunting moose. My son called to me in the tent, "You hear that noise?" It was a big animal [grizzly bear]. When a big animal makes that noise, that sound just goes in you. My brother told me, "Don't send your Old Man or your son out. You go out yourself because big animals are scared of women."

I remembered that, so I went out of the tent. My Old Man and my son were right by the door. I was scared but they were right there with the gun. I turned over a stump on the fire and boy, that light got bright. That animal came right up to our camp again, but that stump was burning and it went away.

My Old Man asked me, "You okay?" I say, "Yeah, but start packing up. We got to leave because it could be way back and still watching." So they pack up and start to load boat real quiet. I was last one to leave. That's the way my brother told me, "Don't get in boat fast. Don't get scared. You got to stand up there."

#########

My son and I went fishing at a place we call "Four Cabin." While we were fishing, a mink came. When we would catch a fish, he would try to get that fish from us. Gee, he's hungry. That mink came at one woman and she hit it with her club and she knocked him out. She caught one mink that day. We had fun with other mink while we were fishing. We didn't try to kill them. Night-time, we could hear them go around the tent. They would try to eat our fish. They were hungry. We come back and we hang all our fish up. There were a lot of mink over there.

#########

Everybody stayed in tents in winter-time down at Old Minto, before they get cabins. We made our own tents. We never used no white man tent. It is nice and warm. We burned wood for heat, and kerosene or candles for light. We made our own candles. We'd braid a wick. If we caught a bear, we used that grease. Those candles were smoky, so we just used them while we were cooking or eating.

#########

We didn't have fishwheels. We set fish net. We had a good spot. My Old Man could tell where there was gravel and fish like that gravel. I make my own nets. We get what they call "canoe canvas." We take it apart and twist the strands and make our own net. It took two months, because I had to do my own twisting. Now, we can buy twine and fix net.

One year, we caught hardly any fish. We had dogs, but nothing to feed them. We stayed in fish camp. My brother-in-law Neal moved us over to his site. We set our net, and boy we started catch fish. We fed those dogs good.

#########

The elders taught us lots of lessons. I work with kids today, and I still use some of those old lessons:
- If we caught squirrels by mistake in our traps, we never threw them away. There is a story about that, too. When they had starvation back in 1937, people fed their kids squirrel. We know all about that because my father-in-law used to talk to us.

- A long time ago, they used to go all the way from Old Minto to Livengood to find moose track. When they found a track, they followed it until they caught the moose. Now, everything is different. We just go out a little ways and see moose.
- One time, me and my Old Man were checking traps. We had seven dogs. We just bumped a tree and busted up the sled. He had to go out right away and look for birch to repair the sled. The elders told us to never wait.
- Long time ago, everybody used to tan their own moose skin. No more. None of the women tan moose skin any more. Nobody tries to make a canoe, either.

Susie and her husband shared important life lessons with their children. At one point, the family needed a new boat and motor. The parents led a family effort to raise the money through trapping. They succeeded and took great pride in the effort.

We wanted a boat and motor, but couldn't afford it. I tell our sons, "We'll go beaver trapping and earn it. That's the only way you guys will learn. If you don't work for wages, you got to learn how to trap." We went across to the other side of the Flats and put up a tent. We were trapping eight dens. We caught eight beaver one night. We also caught lynx and otter.

My son said, "Mom, I'll take the beaver over to the village so our brother Eric can skin them." So, we went to check more sets. They caught four more big beavers. My Old Man said, "We're piling up beavers." The boys would go one way and we'd go the other way. We'd get back and they had a load and we had a load. We said, "We won't take our tent down until we're done." We caught lots of beavers ... big sack.

We went to Persinger's in Fairbanks. We bought boat and motor. We were lucky we get that much money for our fur. We just took care of ourselves. My kids saw it could be done with trapping. They learned a lesson. They did it with us. We did everything with our kids ... everything.

Susie grew up without the amenities that most people consider essential to a modern way of life. Although it was a hard life, she remembers it fondly.

From the time we got married, we start off pretty poor. We didn't know nothing at the beginning, but at the end we got to know everything. We got to know the animals. We found out how we could make a good living out of it. We never waste nothing. If we catch moose, we used everything. If we catch fish, we use everything. Trapping, hunting, fishing was important to us.

We kept having floods in Old Minto. People got tired of it, so they had a meeting among the elders. They picked out three places for us to move. All three places had good fishing and access to all the lakes in Minto Flats. So, they choose right here [New Minto]. We were last one down there. We weren't happy with the choice. Old Minto was good for us. We move over here in August. We all stayed in tent when we first came over here, and we started to build houses.

We used to work hard. We used to burn wood; didn't know nothing about oil, nothing about running water. We packed our own water. We cut our own wood. We didn't have 'hook up' lights. After we moved here, I bought a little generator. We were first one who had TV. Today. I'm sorry I bought it. I didn't know people were going to spend all their time watching TV. That's why the kids don't want to learn nothing.

Even facing the challenges of advancing age, Susie continues to be actively involved in the lives of her children.

Right now, I can't do much. My kids ask me, "Mom, you go with us." I don't want to say no because before my husband died he told me, "Do everything you can with those kids. They need one of us."

• *Athabaskan Indians were taught to avoid saying the word "bear." Susie no longer adheres strictly to that prohibition. However, she often goes back to the old way of referring to a bear as a "big animal."*

• *Susie refers to her late husband as "Old Man." In the Native culture, this is not a sign of disrespect.*

AL WRIGHT
Fairbanks, AK

Al Wright's parents were missionaries. They lived in many small villages throughout Interior Alaska. Al grew to love the region and the lifestyle. His youth was filled with simple activities; idyllic by today's standards. He learned to hunt, fish, and trap at an early age.

I was born at Tanana Crossing in 1925. It was a small Native village. The only way to get there was by boat in the summer or dog team in the winter. My parents were missionary people, so we moved around a lot. A couple of years after I was born, we moved to Nenana. A couple years after that, we moved to Minto. That is where I started hunting. My dad bought me a .22 when I was about six years old. I started out hunting ducks and muskrats.

A guy named Jimmy Bruce showed me how to set traps for mink and muskrat when I was seven years old. I'd go out on weekends and set a few traps for foxes. Towards spring I would try and catch some muskrats.

When I was about nine years old, Jimmy took me on a trip hunting muskrats in March. We went by dog team down to Minto Flats. That's when I learned to eat muskrats. Jimmy didn't take very much food or gear with him. The first day we got there we set up camp and he says, "Let's go see if we can get something to eat." I didn't know how to find the muskrat houses, but he showed me and we set some traps.

About noon he says, "Let's have lunch. You build a fire and put some water on to make tea." We were on our way back from setting traps and we had picked up four or five muskrats. Jimmy picked out a couple good-looking muskrats and told me to skin them. He put them on a stick and put them by the fire. He didn't cut off the tail or the head.

When they were cooked, he handed one to me with a pilot bread cracker and said, "Here's your lunch." He started eating on his. I look[ed] at the teeth and tail and I couldn't quite hack it. After he was done eating, he says, "Well, we better get going." He never said a word about me eating or not eating. By about the third day, I was so hungry I could pick up that muskrat, look him right in the eye, and eat the whole damn thing. That's what you had to eat. If you didn't like it … too bad.

I learned to run equipment when I was a kid. We had a wood saw on an old Model T truck. We went around and sawed firewood for folks. I eventually learned how to run a Cat. During World War II, the government confiscated all the heavy equipment from the miners so they could build airfields. I got a job running a Cat. I was about 16. I worked on the airports at Gulkana, Summit, and Bettles. When they started building the highway to Anchorage, I got put on that job. I was trying to get in the military but they kept giving me deferments to work on these construction jobs. I never got in the Army until about 1944. I got out in June of '46.

Wright also loved airplanes. He learned to fly after serving in World War II. Al bought a small plane almost immediately and launched into his life's work.

Ever since I was a little kid, airplanes fascinated me. I used to meet all the airplanes that landed. The mail plane would come once a week. I snowshoed the runway for them. With the GI Bill, everybody was able to go to school of some sort. I signed up for that and learned to fly. I got a little T-Craft right off the bat. I paid $3,500; brand new. I was 21. We used to park our planes on the Chena [River] right by Samson Hardware.

I started flying trappers. I still remember my first trip. A guy was looking for somebody to pick up his fur. He had been trapping all winter up on the Ladue River. He walked out to Northway and then hitched a ride into Fairbanks. There were all these guys learning to fly, but nobody wanted to go. I said, "I'll do it." That was my first big flying job.

That plane had narrow skis. They'd sink right to the bottom every time I'd land in unpacked snow. So, I'd have to snowshoe a runway. The trapper had all kinds of marten and lynx. We had every corner of that little plane stuffed with fur. After we landed in Fairbanks, he said, "I'll find a furbuyer and then pay you for the trip." That's how I got started flying.

All kinds of trappers figured flying was the way to go. Just prior to the season, I'd stuff their supplies and their dog team in the airplane and then tie the sled on the ski. It was actually cheaper for them to fly out to their cabin than it was to mush out because they'd waste all that trapping time when the season was open. In addition, it would save them a lot of hard work breaking trail.

A long flying career in Alaska is not without a few mishaps. Some of Al's incidents were weather-related, others mechanical in origin. He dealt with all of the accidents in a straight-forward manner, although in ways which the FAA would frown upon today.

I've had some airplane problems.

One year they had to freeze in the riverboat *Nenana* down on the Nowitna River. They hired a guy to take care of it all winter. I'd haul this guy some mail and groceries during the winter and check on him once in a while. Late in the spring, I had to change from skis to wheels because there was no more snow on Weeks Field. I landed at that boat. I had just hauled a load of groceries in to him the day before, so I knew I could land on wheels. There was a little wind blowing and I was having a hard time turning around so I swung out a little bit further into the river than I generally did and god darn, I dropped a wheel through the ice and it bent the prop.

There was a crew of about 20 guys getting the boat ready to go. We took some sheets of plyboard off the boat and threw them underneath the wing. That way, we'd have something to stand on and spread the weight around. We got five or six guys and lifted that wing out of the hole and then shoved a piece of plyboard over the hole. Then they took the propeller off and the boat engineer says, "I can fix that." He stuck the propeller between some braces on the boat and bent it back until it was pretty straight. Then he took a hammer and a block of wood and banged on a few places to straighten the tips a little more. We put it back on and it flew just as good as ever.

Another time, a guy was trying to sell me a Gull Wing Stinson. I had some folks who wanted to go to Nenana. I figured I could take them and check out this airplane at the same time. I had never been in that airplane before. I was in the driver's seat and the seller was coaching me on the other side.

We got a little over halfway to Nenana and oil started showing up on the windshield. It got thicker and thicker. I says, "We are going to have to land this thing. We'll never make it to Nenana." By then, I couldn't see out the windshield at all. There's a little side window with a crank. So I rolled that window down and stuck my head out the side to look around. I saw a sandbar that looked good enough to land on. I turned the airplane around real quick and told the guy to put the flaps down. I didn't even know where the flap handle was. I got it on the ground, but I ground-looped the airplane. It nosed up and then fell back down and it didn't hurt anything. The prop seal had failed and all the oil came out.

I had been talking to the Nenana tower. I told them we were landing on a bar up there and asked if they could get somebody to come get us. Another pilot came down and hauled the passengers to Nenana. He got me a new prop seal, oil, tools, and brought them back down and we put the new seal in. That was back when the FAA had only two guys around here. They had a hard time keeping track of everybody.

In '49, I was flying that same Gull Wing Stinson. I was going to Nenana with one passenger. I was circling town so someone would come out to give us a ride after we landed. We were about 500 feet up. Smoke started coming in the cabin. We were only a mile from the runway, so I started to turn and descend. Almost instantly, the whole inside was full of smoke and flames. We were wearing heavy winter clothes. I pulled the hood of my parka up over my head so I wouldn't get burned. I told my passenger to wrap up in the sleeping bag he was sitting on.

I hollered, "I'm going to try to get to the runway. If we make it, just bail out. It's better than burning up." About that time, I couldn't see the instruments on the panel any more. I figured it was all over. The last thing I saw on the gauges, we were going 130 miles an hour.

We were down to 300 feet. I shut the engine off and tried to hold the plane straight. Then I felt the thing quit flying. The fabric on the wings and fuselage had been sealed with nitrate dope. Once it's exposed to flame, it's just "poof" and it's gone. Without the fabric on the wings, nothing was keeping us flying. We fell at least 200 feet.

We were just nosing in when we hit the trees, so we hit pretty flat. One wing caught a tree and swung the plane sideways down through the trees. It hit the ground, then sheared off the landing gear and came to a stop. I had my belt unhooked and went flying up into the instrument panel and the windshield. I had cuts all over my head. I was pretty well beat up, but I wasn't knocked cold. The fire was all around us. I couldn't figure out how come we were still alive. Everything happened so fast.

I had to go over the back seat to get to the door. I was going to ram my shoulder against the door, but the door was gone and I fell out on the ground. I hollered to this guy I had with me. I never heard a word, so I was feeling around in there trying to find him. Finally, I felt his hand so I grabbed ahold and yanked him out the door. He was wrapped up in that sleeping bag and trying to figure out how to get out of it. I started dragging him away from the airplane. I got maybe five or six feet from the airplane and passed out, colder than a turkey. He was okay, so he got up and dragged me away from the airplane. Of course, there was nothing left of the airplane ... completely burned up.

A doctor happened to be in town. He sewed me all back together. I was all bandaged up. Neither one of us could even move for about a week; we were so beat up from hitting the ground so hard. Luckily, we didn't have any broken bones.

After that incident, I was laid up for about three weeks; couldn't do anything. A couple days before Christmas, this furbuyer from Seattle came along. He wanted to go down to Tolovana. I had a T-Craft, but it was only a $15 trip and it was colder than the devil. It was 50 below and I never flew that plane if it got colder than 30 below because there wasn't enough heat to keep it running good. I needed money so damn bad I agreed to take him. I figured I'd get up to 3,000 feet and it would be warmer. Just about time I got to the end of the runway, the engine quit. I landed within 100 yards of that burned-up Stinson. I didn't wreck the T-Craft very bad. I found a willow patch to land in. When we got out of the plane, the wings were resting on the bent-over willows, and the skis were about 4 feet off the ground. It just ripped a few holes in the fabric, but I was practically out of business. Now, I had both airplanes gone.

Al scrambled to get back in business. A new partnership led to some interesting travel and fascinating people. The clientele included trappers.

There was a guy from Koyukuk, Rutsabeck was his name. He had just wrecked his airplane. He was in Nenana trying to figure out what to do. We were both broke. We decided to go in partners and rent an airplane from Fred Sultan. He didn't really want to rent the airplane to two guys who just wrecked their own airplanes, but he finally did. We started Nenana Air Service and built it up. We had lots of business. Within a year, we owned nine airplanes and had several guys flying for us.

We stationed one of our planes at Koyukuk because it was a headquarters for that part of the Yukon. There was a trader there by the name of Dominic Vernetti. He would outfit a bunch of trappers each winter. Vernetti would pay for their air charters, too. Then, he would collect from the trappers. So you never worried about getting your money. We had trappers from Ruby and Galena and Koyukuk and Nulato scattered all over the country.

Just before Christmas, Dominic would make a trip to all the trapping camps. He'd collect all the fur and send it off to auction houses Outside. He'd keep enough of the money to pay the bills that all these people owed him. The remainder, he'd give to the trappers. Every once in a while, one of them would decide he didn't want to pay his bill. He'd get another plane to take him to Ruby or Fairbanks to sell his fur. Then, he'd blow all his money and Dominic wouldn't get repaid.

Vernetti treated those people pretty good. Some of the missionaries and other do-gooders thought the traders were real bad people and taking advantage of the Indians. Most of them weren't. They were honest people. They'd make sure the locals had food for the whole year (on credit) and then they would get it all back after the trapping season. In the summer, all the locals would be in fish camps. They would dry and bale fish. Vernetti had a little barge and a boat. He'd buy the fish from them for 5 cents a pound. He stored it in a big warehouse. In the winter, he would sell it back to them for their dogs for ten cents a pound.

In addition to trappers, Al flew furbuyers, too. Once again, he worked with very colorful characters.

I also started flying furbuyers around. I flew Muskrat Johnny [Schwegler] quite a bit. He was an old weaseled-up little guy that worked for the New York Fur Exchange. He knew everybody in the whole state. He had traveled all over this country by dog team before the War. After he started flying with me, he didn't use dogs any more.

The big furbuyers would make their rounds to all these traders. I used to take Schwegler and Goldberg and another a guy named Jacobson. They called him Walrus Jake, because he had a big mustache. There were probably six or seven different furbuyers that would make the rounds just before Christmas and then again in the spring. They'd try to outbid each other on the fur. Schweigler would always try to stay at Hughes because they had a good roadhouse there. Dominic had a good place to stay in Koyukuk, too. He was a fat little Italian guy and he cooked really good meals.

In those days, we didn't have fast communication so the village traders wouldn't know what the latest fur prices were. The furbuyers knew about price changes because they could telegraph or telephone to Seattle or New York just before they left on a buying trip. Sometimes there would be three or four of the big furbuyers at the same place at the same time. They were all trying to outfox each other on the price.

One year, after the 'rat season, Schwegler wanted to go to Kotzebue. I had never been to Kotzebue before. Schwegler says, "No problem. I've been over that route lots of times. I can show you the way." We did our business at Hughes and headed for Kotzebue.

As we were flying along, Johnny would look out the window and say, "We're right on course." Then we'd get to places he didn't recognize and he would pretend he was asleep. I would ask, "Johnny, where are we?" He wouldn't move. Finally, he'd recognize a mountain or a river and say, "We're doing fine." We didn't get to Kotzebue until about two o'clock in the morning. As we were coming in, a fog bank was rolling in, too. If we couldn't beat the fog bank, we were in trouble because I didn't have enough gas to go anyplace else. So I had the throttle wide open, diving for that pond. We made it.

I headed to Ferguson's Hotel. Johnny says, "If Jake is there, don't tell him you brought me. I'm going over to Rockman's Store." Jake was staying at the hotel. Jake sees me come in and says, "Did you bring Johnny?" I says, "I don't know what you're talking about. I'm tired. I've been flying all night. I'm going to bed." He kept pestering me. I wouldn't tell him, but he knew damn well I brought Johnny.

The locals had taken a lot of muskrats that year and the price was high. In the morning, Johnny bought Rockman's 'rats ... all 60,000 of them. Jake had been there for about a week, trying to buy those 'rats. He started out low and offered a little more each day. The day before we got there he raised the price 5 cents a 'rat and said, "That's my final price. If you don't take it, I'm leaving tomorrow." When Johnny got in and bought all of the fur, Jake was just madder than hell, "God damn, you sneak Johnny in here and he buys the fur out from under me" and one thing and another.

When we got back to Fairbanks, Johnny told me to come down to the Nordale Hotel the next day and he would pay me for the trip. I went down there and I start walking up to the room. I hear somebody in the room. They're talking and laughing. I stop and listen for a while. Hell, it's Jake in there with him. They're laughing about how they got all this fur at such a great price. As soon as I knocked on the door, everything changed. Jake says, "God damn you, Johnny. You went and bought that fur out from under me. You so and so." Like they were bitter enemies. Jake left as I walked in. Johnny mumbled some bad things about Jake, but I know darn well they were in cahoots on that deal.

Spring-time in the Interior is muskrat hunting season. 'Rats provided a reliable source for locals to make some money.

In the spring at Minto, I'd tie a canoe on the side of the float and fly guys out to a lake. There were creeks and channels all over those Flats. When the water was high in the spring, you could paddle almost any place. Most of the time, three or four guys would travel together, but I could only haul one at a time. I would dump them off on a lake about 20 miles away and they would paddle back hunting muskrats along the way. They'd skin them out and save the bodies for their dogs. Their wives were doing all the stretching and final pelt preparation. They'd pay all their fares with 'rats. I hauled groceries down there and trade them for 'rats.

When it would get hot in the summer, that plane would stink like hell. Muskrats don't smell bad, but they do have an odor. In addition, we'd haul moose meat in the fall and seal pokes full of seal oil. Of course, those pokes always leaked a little. You mix all those together and it got pretty strong.

The muskrat season was open until the 1st of June. They'd trap 'rats first and then when the water opened up they'd start shooting them. Toward the middle or end of May, the hunters would get together and evaluate the harvest and remaining population. They'd say, "The number of muskrats is down where we should leave them alone. We've got to leave the rest to repopulate for next year. We're going to quit hunting 'rats on such and such day." Legally, they could still go hunting, but they quit. They regulated it themselves and there were always enough 'rats.

When I was flying, I'd haul 10,000 muskrats out of Minto Flats every year. When the price went down, nobody hunted them anymore. The muskrats died off. You couldn't hardly find a muskrat down there. To this day, there are very few muskrats. You've got to harvest those animals at a certain amount or they will go to pot.

The residents of Minto village grew tired of annual spring floods. They eventually decided to relocate the village.

The old village of Minto flooded every year. They wanted to move to higher ground. They had a vote to decide where to go. They decided on the North Fork site. After the vote, they had to figure out how to get a village started there. There was a sawmill across the river from Old Minto. When it came time to move the village, they started up the sawmill again. They were going to make cabin logs and lumber to build their own houses. The Bureau of Indian Affairs had a program where each family could get $3,000 to put into a house. $3,000 would buy all the doors and windows you needed and you could build some nice houses. We thought that was a really great plan.

Then Alaska Housing came along and said, "No, no, no. We're going to build frame houses." So they had this big meeting. God, they were arguing back and forth. They finally decided to leave it up to the people which way they wanted to go. Most of the people wanted to live like white men ... in a frame house. So Alaska Housing won out. They built all those cracker box houses sitting on stilts.

They could have ended up with a nice house for each family, and it wouldn't have cost them a penny. They would have owned them outright, free of debt. Instead, Alaska Housing charged them $8,000 for those cracker boxes. Of course, they never made the payments. Eventually, they tore them all down and built log houses, with logs shipped in from Canada. That's our government.

Wright played a pivotal role in the first road from the Interior up to the North Slope.

I scouted the first trail up to Prudhoe in the early '60s. Old Tennessee Miller had some Cats and other equipment he took up there on the first trip. We went up from Dunbar to Livengood and over to Stevens Village and then across the Yukon River by the Dall and cross into the Jim River and the Koyukuk and then up the John River past Anaktuvuk and on down about halfway to Umiat and then turned off to the right and went over to Prudhoe Bay. That trail eventually led to the discovery of oil at Prudhoe.

Al had a hand in many activities. Big game guiding was one of his favorites. His flying and guiding activities helped him develop a keen understanding of the biological forces which drive increases and decreases in moose population abundance.

I did a lot of guiding. I went up polar bear hunting a couple of years, but I didn't like it. It was a dangerous sport. You have to land on the ice and it would be moving all the time. You had to know how to tell if a lead was frozen good enough to land on. The way to tell is to slowly taxi along and keep looking back at your tracks. If moisture showed up in the tracks, you got out of there. If there was no water in the tracks, you could stop but you never got out of the airplane right away. You'd sit in there for a minute or so to see if the ice was settling. If water started coming up around the skis, then you goosed it and got the hell out of there.

I knew one kid that went through the ice and drowned. He landed to go after a bear. There was a second airplane traveling with him. They saw him go through the ice. They found a safe place to land about a half a mile away. They ran down there as quick as they could, but the plane and the pilot were gone. The passenger was still floating in the hole. They got a rope to him and drug him out. The only reason he floated is he was wearing down underwear and down pants and a down parka. All those feathers held enough air to keep him afloat. That's the only person I know that was lost, but there were two or three other planes that dropped through the ice. A couple others had mechanical trouble. They went back to town for parts and a mechanic. When they came back to fix it, they couldn't find the plane because it drifted away. That ice is always moving.

I broke a landing gear out there on the ice one day, but it didn't collapse. I had about 10 cans of gas with me. I unloaded all the gas and piled it in a pyramid so I could see it from quite a ways. Then I got a rope and tied the landing gear together so it couldn't collapse. I took off all right and got back to Barrow with my hunter. I couldn't find anybody to weld the gear, so I eventually welded it myself. It was only about 15 miles out of Barrow where this happened. I had a good "fix" on Barrow with a VOR, so I knew the exact course and how long it took to fly back. It was two days before I got back out there and I never did find that gas pile. It drifted away.

A lot of times you'd fly around and you'd see your old tracks where you landed the day before. Some of them would be going this way and some of it would be going that way. The ice had busted up and refroze.

Polar bear weren't the only wildlife hunted from the air. Even the federal government got in the act.

There hadn't been a moose on the north side of the Brooks Range. The feds had five airplanes with a gunner and a pilot. They killed lots of wolves that way. According to Fish & Wildlife, those five airplanes shot 350 wolves. There were probably seven or eight private guys hunting up there, too.

They got at least 100 wolves apiece. So they obviously thinned the wolf population down pretty good. Then the moose population started to come back and then the moose migrated across onto the North Slope.

I hunted up there, too. There's an area on the western North Slope called the Naval Petroleum Reserve. During World War II, they were doing seismic work up there. They made gas caches all over the country, 80 octane aviation gas. Then they discontinued the exploration program and abandoned the equipment and caches. When you'd go up there, you didn't have to worry about gasoline. You'd just find the caches, take whatever gas you needed to fill your airplane, and go hunting again.

I also did a lot of moose hunting. In the '40s, there were hardly any moose around Fairbanks. In the 1950s, the federal Fish & Wildlife Service came in and started killing wolves. They dropped poison bait all over the country. Of course, they killed everything else in addition to wolves ... foxes and wolverines and bears and anything that would eat the baits. There was a lot of criticism about that.

By the '60s, there were a lot of moose around the Fairbanks area. When they were building the Air Force station at Clear, I was flying a crew of about 10 guys down to Clear in the morning and back to Fairbanks at night. It was a 20-minute flight. Just for something to do, they'd count moose. If they didn't count 100 moose between Clear and here, there was something wrong.

There were moose all over this country. In those days you could fly and shoot the same day. We'd take moose hunters out to lakes all around the area. We guaranteed them a moose landed in Fairbanks for $150.

I had a hunting camp just out of Gold King. It was a moose hunter's paradise. You could sit on the hill and count 100 bull moose from one spot. I guided moose hunters out there for about 10 years. We'd take maybe 10 or 12 moose out of my camp every year.

This little valley had probably 50 cows and calves and there was a little band of caribou, too. Then, they opened up a season for cows and calves that extended into November. There was no snow that year and you could drive a four-wheel drive pick-up from Clear into Gold King. I went out there just to protect my camp. These hunters came in and killed every animal in that little valley by my camp. There wasn't one left when they got done.

We had super heavy snow that winter. We'd start doing surveys as the snow melted down in the spring. We counted over 100 dead moose from Eielson up to the head of the Chena, mostly calves. They starved to death. The snow was so deep they stuck to trails because it was easier walking. All the moose were using the same trails and they ate up everything. By spring, it wiped out over half the moose in the central Interior. So then they shortened the season. You were still allowed to kill a bull but they were hard to find. I remember one trip to Minto Flats. I flew six hours and found one cow moose.

When I was in this guiding business they used to allot you certain areas to hunt. Bill Waugaman wanted part of my area near the Wood River. The Board had just taken the license away from another guide who had an area just past mine by the Totalanika River. I agreed to let Bill have part of my area if they would give me this other parcel. They agreed to it. Of course, this was all verbal during the meeting. When it came time to put it on the paper, they wouldn't do it. They gave Waugaman part of my area, but they wouldn't give me this other area. I got so damn mad I says, "Here's your damn guide license. Do whatever you want with it. I don't want it anymore." I quit guiding.

Al is the quintessential Alaskan, with years of adventure behind him. He is a soft-spoken, hard-working man who has accomplished much. Al lists his favorite places and activities in the Great Land.

I've flown all over this state. For scenic value, the Gates of the Arctic is the most unique place I've seen. I used to take tourists around Mt. McKinley. That was a good scenic flight, too. I also still like Minto Flats. I guess that's because I grew up there. I still have a cabin down there, just off the Big Lake. Hunting and fishing were always my main recreations. I was always fishing or hunting whenever I could.

RON LONG
Fairbanks, AK

Ron Long grew up in Oklahoma. He started trapping coyotes and bobcats when he was eight years old. The U.S. Air Force brought Ron to Interior Alaska and he never left.

There was a pretty good variety trapping in Oklahoma. The biggest thing was coyotes. We used to get $3.50 a head for the bounty. It made spending money, especially when I was in high school. I came to Alaska in 1956 with the Air Force. I always wanted to come up here, even when I was a little kid. The adventure of Alaska intrigued me.

Ron's early years of trapping in Alaska were both fun and productive. In the first few years, he focused on mink and beaver. In later years, Ron switched his emphasis to fox, lynx and wolves. He became an expert on all species.

I started trapping around Fairbanks. The population at that time was around 12,000. There was a lot of fur and there wasn't very much competition. The big money in those days was beaver and mink. Beaver were bringing $50 and a big male mink was bringing $30. Gas at that time was fifty cents a gallon.

One year, I was trapping out of an old wall tent. There were shrews all over. I don't mean one or two ... I mean THOUSANDS of shrews. Those damn shrews crawled up the tent wall, backlit by the moonlight, just like a horror story. They'd get up high enough that they couldn't hold on any more. Then they fell right down into your sleeping bag! I rolled over and squashed a few of them. Or have them run across your face. God, that was fun!

One time, I didn't have enough money to buy traps. I said to Norm Phillips, "You buy half of these traps and I'll show you how to trap!" We'd trap beaver together in the springtime. We brought in a lot of beaver. The big problem with beaver is you have to skin them. Man, that was a chore.

In the early years, Ron used a dog team for trapline transportation.

At the time, there wasn't any other way to go. We didn't start getting snow machines until the 1970s. Everybody that was trapping had a dog team. They ranged from two or three dogs up to nine dogs. The average trapper would put twenty miles on his dog team per day. Dogs can haul a lot of gear and weight, especially if you have a good trail.

I had some pretty good dogs. I had an advantage over most people. My brother-in-law raised some awful good dogs and he lived right next to me. The key thing in training a dog team for a trapline is the leader. I trained them for competition, too. My daughter was racing dogs at that time. I didn't let my dogs "tritty trot." They ran all the way! When we went from one set to another, we RAN. There wasn't any playing. I could actually go some places faster with dogs than I could with a snowmachine. On a real winding trail, dogs will beat a snowmachine.

Dogs had their advantages and disadvantages. One disadvantage was that you had to feed them during the summer. Another thing was that you had to GET that feed. We had a fairly cheap source of feed and that was fish. In the fall, you could go out on the Tanana with a net, and get enough fish for your dogs for the whole year.

Another big disadvantage to dogs was deep snow! If you got 2 foot of snow in one dump, you were done. Then you started snowshoeing in front of the dogs. It kept you in shape, I'll tell you that. We'd try to get two guys working together. One guy would run on snowshoes ahead of the dogs. The other guy would hold the dogs. When he started mushing, he would catch up with the first guy pretty quickly. They would switch places and just alternate that way back and forth.

There are dog men and then there's people that use snow machines. They can turn that snow machine off in the spring and not worry about it until the fall.

Ron knows first-hand the early snowmachines weren't always reliable. He shares a few horror stories.

When the snow machines came out, that was really a God-send. But there's one bad thing about snowmachines. Just when you think you're safe ... you break down. There goes an axle, or something else you couldn't fix. One time, Pete Buist was riding tandem with me. We were at the far end of my 'line and the axle goes BOOM! We started walking at about 3 o'clock in the afternoon. It seemed like we walked 150 miles!

I remember another time I broke down and had to walk back. That was probably the longest I ever walked. I would walk until I got tired and then take a rest. Walk and rest. By the time I finally got to the cabin I was only walking 50 yards before I had to sit down. I was completely worn out.

If your 'line is anywhere near water, you are going to get into overflow. I've broken through my share. When you put a snowmachine in water, it takes all the life out of it. I always carried winches. If the machine wasn't stuck too bad, I could get it out.

Trapping was the primary focus of Ron's life. After a few years trapping around Fairbanks, a co-worker suggested Ron check out the fur prospects south of Fairbanks. That advice turned out to be a life-changer. He trapped the area for more than 30 years.

In the early years, I trapped everywhere. One year, a friend of mine told me there were a lot of mink over on the Tanana Flats. It didn't look like it does today. There wasn't a single human track a mile south of the Tanana River.

The first few years, we stayed in wall tents. We trapped primarily mink and beaver. That's where the money was and that's what we concentrated on. When snow machines came along, our mink catches starting increasing. We covered a lot more country and we caught a lot more animals. Between the good years, you'd have those down periods where there was hardly any mink at all. Sometimes, there wasn't any feed to support them.

One year, it seemed like lynx fell out of the sky. There were tracks everywhere. Lynx weren't bringing too much, maybe $60 or $70. We wound up with 270 lynx that season. You have to remember we didn't have any competition. I don't put in a lot of sets, either. When I was catching those big lynx numbers, the maximum number of lynx sets I put in was 100. I've been on traplines where there were so many traps, you couldn't even put your foot down. If you look for "quality" places to put your trap, you'll catch your animals.

There were a lot of fox on the Tanana Flats back then. It was nothing to come home with 20 fox on the sled. There were a number of years when I averaged over 100 fox. There were a lot of voles in that country at that time. If you have a lot of voles and not a lot of snow you got a heck of a fox population. We used to have a tremendous fox population over there and we don't have it any more. I don't know why.

In my area, there seems to be a lot of fur, maybe even more than in the past. We have a fairly good wolf population. We have a fairly good lynx population and this year we had a tremendous mink population.

I don't care where you trap, you don't want to put traplines too close together. People have a tendency to do that. I figure if you can keep seven miles between 'lines, then you can pretty well control the fur populations. When you start overlapping, then you're asking for trouble. You're going to see your populations drop, especially the marten population. If you get two or three guys picking at marten, you'll knock 'em right out.

To be successful, a trapper must understand animal behavior. Ron became a successful wolf trapper. He recalls his favorite wolf story.

I'm not a big wolf trapper. We've caught a few over there. We were sitting in the cabin one night and it was real quiet. We could hear a wolf howling. I said, "With those wolves howling, I wonder if we got a few. We put a lot of traps over there. Tomorrow we'll go over and look." We had seven wolves in the traps. They were all on steel drags with eight foot of chain. The drag marks crossed over each other. You couldn't tell where they were going. We eventually found all but one. It busted the wood toggle. I said, "Well, that one's gone."

This is the story of that one that got away. Maybe three weeks later, I'm about 15 miles south of the cabin. I always used an old moose antler as an attractant at a set. Every animal that came by would urinate on that antler. As I went by, I looked back where the trap was located. I could see that something had disturbed it, but I couldn't tell what it was. I had my .22 with me. I go in there and here's this wolf. Most wolves, when you walk up to them, they're docile. This one was watching me. I took the gun out and just about the time I was ready to squeeze off, he jumped at me. The only thing that stopped him from getting me was that chain and drag. He hit the end of that chain and swung back around. You talk about being scared. I emptied that pistol as fast as I could. That was the only aggressive wolf I've ever seen.

Ron was a flamboyant story-teller. He loved a funny story, even if he was the butt of the joke.

Jim Wendell had just come back from Vietnam when I met him. He was shaky from his experiences in the war. He wanted to go trapping with me and I said sure. One time, it's about 30 or 40 below out there. We were in the cabin after a day on the 'line. I'm sitting in one chair and he's sitting in a chair across the cabin. I had this .22 pistol. I take out the clip and put it on a shelf above the stove. Both the pistol and the clip had snow inside. I got the receiver back and I'm trying to get snow out of it. All of a sudden, PAH WOOM!

I looked across the cabin and saw Wendell kinda double over. As he's going down he says, "You shot me." He thought he made it all the way through Vietnam and now I just about killed him in a little trapping cabin in Alaska. I looked at this pistol and the receiver's still back.

All of a sudden BOOM BOOM BOOM!! I don't know where they're coming from. So I ran out of the cabin. Then it went BOOM BOOM and I ran back in. I didn't know who or what was shooting. As soon as I settled down, I saw what happened. The snow forced those bullets out of the clip and they fell down on top of the stove. The first one, the side of the case blew out and a piece imbedded in Wendell's hand. Part of it was still sticking out. I said, "I think I can cut that damn thing out."

He says, "God no, don't do that."

I says, "What are we going to do?"

He says, "We gotta get back to town."

I said, "It's 40 below out there."

He says, "I don't care how cold it is. You get that snowmachine going. I'll hang on."

I says, "With one hand?"

He says, "Yeah, I'll hang on."

It was one of those old Ski Doos. It froze up every 20 miles. You had to take a torch to thaw out the carburetor. So here we go. I'm riding this thing and he's on the sled, holding on with a one-hand death grip! We made it back to town and he never fell off. He never wanted to trap with me again. Can't imagine why.

In addition to trapping, Ron bought fur for many years.

When I was buying fur, guys would bring in foxes and I would refer to them as "foot rags." That offended some people. That phrase came from Fort Yukon. The Natives up there would use poor-quality fur to wrap their boots. That's where the term "foot rag" came from. One of the guys in Fort

Yukon started using that phrase and I kinda stole it from him.

Trappers are funny when it comes to the value of their fur. They'd be sitting in their cabin, with ten to 15 marten on the wall. Every time they went by that fur, they'd pet it. Every time they pet it, it went up $5. By the time he got to me, every one of those marten was worth $150.

I'd ask, "What do you think it's worth? Write it down. I'll write down a price, too. We'll see how close we are."

You would be surprised at the prices you'd get! Buying fur was quite an adventure. I never made any money at it.

Long was one of several trappers instrumental in forming the Alaska Trappers Association. He served on the Board of Directors and received the Fabian Carey Trapper of the Year award in 1997.

Fabian Carey was a very nice man, very helpful to other trappers. He'd bring in some awful big catches of marten from the Minchumina country. I was kind of fascinated with that 'cause at that time there weren't many marten around this country.

Fabian is considered the Father of the Alaska Trappers Association. Several of us talked about forming an organization. We knew we were in trouble 'cause the antis were starting to make inroads into Alaska. We knew we had to organize. It started as just a bunch of trappers and we hoped something good would happen. And it did! A lot of people put a lot of time in this thing in the early days. We had no idea it would last as long as it has or was going to be as strong as it is now.

Long loved to hunt moose. He shot his share of big ones.

About 1961, I was guiding for moose over in the foothills of the Alaska Range. Clients usually shared meat, but not this year. All of the clients had taken the meat from their animals and I needed some meat. I'm looking around and here's the biggest bull I ever saw. This bull is in full rut and he's a huge son of a gun! I says, "Oh God! I'd like to kill that thing, but I need the meat more than I need the antlers." To make a long story short, I killed another one. The next year, I'm at almost the same place; it was a month earlier. I'm glassing across the valley. This country has a lot of uprooted trees, with roots sticking up. I see this great big root ball and then all of a sudden it moved!

I says, "Holy mackerel, there that baby is again. He's not getting away this time!" It was a long ways over there. "BOOM," I shot and up he jumps and runs away. I said a prayer and "BOOM," touched off another one. Missed him again. I finally got him with the third shot. As I'm walking over there and I knew he was close to the world record. It was about 2 miles to the air-strip. I look across the valley and here's another moose. Yep ... I did. Shot that one, too. Boy, you talk about packing out some moose meat. That first moose was number 19 in the record book. He was a magnificent moose. The rack was 72 inches wide and had brow palms that were wide on both sides. That country was good for moose.

Ron pulls no punches regarding his priorities.

The outdoors has been my life. I always had a heck of a time. I've gone through a couple marriages. Women were second, the outdoors came first. That's a pretty rash statement. My kids still go with me up into the mountains. Alaska has been very good to me and I hope it continues to be good to me for a couple more years.

{RON LONG PASSED AWAY IN 2003}

KEN DEARDORFF
McGrath, AK

Ken Deardorff grew up in California, far removed from the natural world. He dreamed of living in the Far North. After college, Ken moved to Alaska and homesteaded on a remote river south of McGrath.

I had an uncle who gave me a subscription to Field & Stream when I was four years old. Every month (before I could even read), I would stare at the cover and try to determine which way was north in that picture. I devoured those magazines every month. About the time I was seven, I read a book called "Crusoe of Lonesome Lake." The guy was homesteading in 1900 in British Columbia. That really got me pointed north and set my sites on eventually getting to Alaska.

I moved up and homesteaded on the Stony River. That was also the first year I trapped. I never saw a trap or snare growing up in California. It wasn't a real successful year. I think I caught one mink, one marten, one beaver, and one ermine. I was out there every single day trying. It got kind of discouraging day after day after day, walking seven or eight miles and not catching anything.

While living in a small nylon tent in February, Ken built a small cabin. When his wife arrived, they immediately embarked on constructing another, larger cabin. It proved to be a real challenge.

We cut and peeled most of the logs right in the immediate area. We'd hook a rope onto them and each pull and drag it to the river bank. When we had several there, we pushed them all in the river, "corralled" them with the canoe, and then rafted them down to where we wanted them. Then we had to reverse the process and pull them all up to the cabin site by hand or by come-along. It was a slow, slow job getting them all there.

Getting the logs up on the wall was another job for the come-along and I only had one. I would have to come-along one end of each log part-way up, tie it off and then go get the other end up. At first, I could maybe make one 'round' of logs per day when the walls were low. As things progressed and got higher and higher, I was down to one log per day rather than a full round per day. I think we finally moved into that particular cabin in December. It was chinked with moss. We were chinking it in November and December. We had to shovel away snow and find moss and scrape it up with a shovel. We hauled it into the cabin we were living in, in order to thaw it out and chink the walls of the other place.

We made some mistakes, but it was still good times. It would have been better if I had more tools. I was limited by what I had been able to bring with me. And of course ... no electricity. The only power tool was a chain saw. If I could sum up homesteading in one thought, it would be that you are constantly taking something apart to get a bolt that will fit something else to fix it long enough to do a job! You just never have the right stuff, or something would break and no way to repair it. No facilities to weld. Just a jar of junk nuts and bolts would have been real handy to have. But pretty tough to get that stuff out there. Everything had to be hauled in either by air or up the river and you are pretty limited as to what you can put in a small boat to get up the river.

In the years that followed, Ken and his young family lived an adventurous lifestyle. Life in Bush Alaska is tough. Sometimes, the critters come a little too close.

One summer morning, I woke up and could hear breathing outside the wall of the cabin! I got my rifle, looked out and there was a black bear right there. I opened the door and the bear stood up. He was about 12 feet from me. I shot him as he lunged toward the door. I jumped back in and slammed the door. He fell and was lying in a heap in front of the door. I waited 30 seconds and opened the door. He was clearly dead.

As I stepped out, another bear ran from behind the cabin. He was 16 or 18 feet from me and I shot that bear! And as soon as that bear was on the ground I heard sort of a "woof." I turned and there was another one standing behind me, about 15 feet away. I shot that one, too.

In the course of 60 seconds, I've got three bears on the ground. They were all within 30 feet. Then I heard a Super Cub. I looked up and here's the Fish and Wildlife Protection Officer circling the cabin. I was motioning for him to come on down and give me a hand with these bears. He just waggled his wings and flew off. About two hours later he showed back up and landed.

His question was, "Do you have them all taken care of yet?"

I said, "Yeah, I do, but you can help me get them to the boat?"

He says, "What are you going to do with them?"

I says, "I can't use that much meat. I'll take 'em to one of the villages and distribute the meat down there."

He helped me pack them down to the boat and I took them to Stony River.

A moose shot at dark one evening attracted an unwanted visitor overnight and surprised the hunters when they returned to the carcass the next morning.

One autumn, a friend and I were hunting moose in a canoe up a little creek. We were coming back down in the evening, and it was just light enough to shoot. We came around a bend and there was a great big bull getting out of the creek. I shot him. Rick and I tied up the canoe and made a fire so we could at least see to gut the thing. Our tent was set up around the very next bend. We gutted the moose and paddled on down to the tent. The next morning, we went back to finish the job. I'm pulling into the bank and Rick has the rope in one hand. He reaches up to grab the base of an alder to tie the boat up and a black bear hangs its head over the cut bank right in front of him,

Rick turned to me and says, "Rifle!!" His face was as white as a sheet. The first thing that came to my hand was a pole and I just pushed the boat away from the bank. By this time, the bear was standing straight up. The bank was probably eight feet high and the bear on top of that, it looked like King Kong was about to jump into the boat. Eventually I tossed Rick his rifle, and he shot the bear. We cut up the bear within 15 feet of the moose. That was a pretty productive hunt.

There's only one real rule in the Bush – survive. Survival means having the right equipment, gear, and supplies at all times. It's necessary to make arrangements for re-supply when at a remote camp for long periods of time. If that re-supply plane doesn't come, things can go bad real fast.

One year, a friend and I were trapping at Whitefish Lake. We'd gone out there in September and another guy was supposed to bring another airplane load of supplies around the first of November. He never showed up. We were getting low on supplies. We'd been out trapping and hunting every day and there was just nothing to eat in the country. I eventually found an old pair of caribou antlers on the beach. I packed those back to the tent and we sawed them into little pieces and boiled them for three days. Eventually there was a little greasy scum that appeared on the top of the water and I figured, "It's got to be clean. It can't hurt."

We had maybe two cups of Krusteaz pancake mix and a little bit of sugar. It wasn't great but I thought it was at least edible. The next morning, Rick was very, very sick. He tried to run his trapline and just couldn't do it. He couldn't keep anything down and couldn't keep anything in. Not that we really had anything to eat, but no matter what he put in his mouth, it was coming right back out, including his teeth. He started losing teeth. By this time, it was probably 12 or 13 days after we had eaten this concoction. I felt okay, just hungry all the time. We finally broke down and starting eating marten. You think marten smells bad while it's cooking, it tastes every bit that bad! But at least it was something in your stomach. Hopefully I'll never have to do that again. I still felt okay but Rick was getting worse by the day.

There was no way to contact anyone. We didn't have any radio and this was before satellite phones. Late one afternoon, maybe an hour before dark, two things happened. A band of about 30 caribou ran out on a lake and I shot one. And a Super Cub flew over. The people landed and I told them what the situation was. They gave me their freeze-dried food. We fixed that up and it seemed to get Rick plugged up. I asked the pilot to call the Fish & Wildlife Protection Officer in McGrath. The weather was bad enough that we didn't see anybody for about ten days, but he eventually showed up. He hauled me out of there. I got to my homestead and made arrangements to get a plane-load of food over to Rick. He decided no matter how bad he felt, he still wanted to stay. I left him the food and I had to return back home.

At the start of one trapping season, Ken had a unique interaction with a pack of wolves near his trapping cabin. It defied expectations based on years of experience in the area.

Years ago, I was standing on the river bank, right at freeze-up. I looked upriver, and saw three wolves coming down on the far side. I knew they were eventually going to hit this opening about 100 yards across the river. I lined up on the opening, and when the first one stepped into the opening, I shot it. Of course, the other two ran back into the brush. I sat there for a few more minutes to make sure that wolf didn't get up. Lo and behold, another wolf walked out of the brush and started to eat the first one. So, I shot the second one. Within 60 seconds, a third one walked out and started eating the first one and I shot that one, too.

I was starting to get wet sitting there in the wet snow. I thought, "I'll go up and dry out and get some warmer clothes." I stood by the stove for maybe a half an hour and went back down to the river. Another wolf steps out of the brush and I shot that one. I was beginning to think, "Where's this going to end?" Eventually a fifth one stepped out and I shot that one, too.

They were all within six or seven feet of one another. I couldn't cross the river to get them. As cold as it was, I figured they would be fine 'til morning. I figured I could get across the next day.

The next morning I was down there at first light, and there were two more wolves sitting there. A big gray one obviously had a full belly. They had been eating on these carcasses from the day before. I shot that one and it went right down. The other wolf jumped back into the brush, but then came out again and I shot that one also.

I had never seen wolves in those numbers before. I thought, "This is just a fluke." But it wasn't a fluke. It continued most of the winter. I managed to trap and snare another ten. All but one of those was within 200 yards of that spot. I got 17 out of that bunch and I thought that I pretty much reduced this pack to where it's probably not a threat. But they killed a moose a quarter mile from the cabin in February. Quite an influx of wolves.

Like many trappers, Ken has run 'lines using both dog sleds and snowmachines. Both offer unique advantages and disadvantages.

I started out running a dog team on the trapline. I had a couple of great dogs from Lime Village. I built a team out of those dogs. Trapping with a dog team, I could tell what was going on in the country a little bit better than with a snowmachine. I had more time to read all the tracks as I was going by.

In terms of reliability, there is no comparison between dogs and snow machines. Dogs always "start." It doesn't matter what the temperature is. I've had to take my dogs across creeks that have opened up. In the spring, the ice would move out of a slough when you're on one side of it and you have to get to the other side. The dogs will certainly do it. They don't like doing it. I didn't like doing it either, but you had to get to the other side if you wanted to get home. You're gonna be wet, but at least you're going to get there. With a snow machine, you'll never get there.

Dogs are company, too. It's a lot nicer to camp in the middle of nowhere with a dog team than it is with a snow machine. It's even nice to bring them into the tent if it's a real cold night. I've had my wife and stepdaughter out on the 'line on real cold nights. We'd bring a dog or two in and pile them next to the kid's sleeping bag. Keep her a little bit warmer. At our cabin, I used to try and bring in one dog every day at least for a few minutes. We called it "Dog of the Day." It created a situation where if one dog got loose, it wouldn't run off, it would run to the door. They'd want to come in, 'cause they knew they'd get some attention or a little special treat to eat.

With a snowmachine, sure it's nice to shut it off and not worry about it. That's the drawback with dogs. You spend all summer either working to buy dog food or go fishing to feed them all winter. With 13 dogs, that took a lot of fish. You're into a 20-hour day, cutting fish and cutting smudge wood and keeping the smudge burning and keeping the flies out of the smokehouse. The snowmachine is easier but I still would much prefer to trap with dogs.

Working with the dogs so intimately, Ken grew to understand their abilities. Perhaps a dog's biggest asset is its nose.

In the fall, I would start from the east end of my 'line and head for the cabin in the center. There was no blazed trail. Some years, the only way I found that trail is my lead dog. I remember one time in particular, the trail went to my left and my dog wanted to go to the right. I stopped him and hauled him back onto the other trail. He immediately jumped off to the right side of the trail again. I stopped him and made him get back on the trail. He immediately jumped off to the right. Finally I thought, "Why fight it?" I let him go to the right!

There was probably a foot and a half of snow and the dogs were having to break trail. Within 200 yards, we intersected the trail we would have eventually arrived at had I gone left. There was a loop in the trail the previous year. My lead dog realized there was a short-cut, but I didn't. He saved me about a half-mile of travel. How he knew that, I don't know. Maybe he could smell that trail was over there. I did notice on the occasions when we would start out in the fall with no trail, he would occasionally stop and lift his head and sniff around and then decide, "Okay it's this way." He was always right! Always right! I had to learn to accept there were times he did know more about what we were doing than I did. It's a pleasure to trap with a good dog team.

Kodiak and Bristol Bay

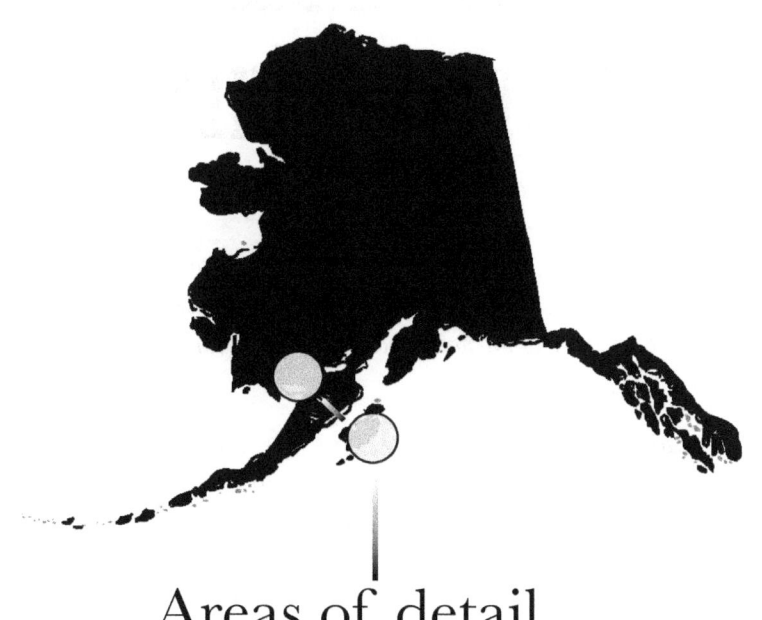

Areas of detail

Ninilchik, Kodiak, Dillingham

DARRELL FARMEN
Ninilchik, AK

Darrell Farmen grew up in western Montana. He came to Alaska right out of high school to work for famous Kodiak bear guides Bill Pinnell and Morris Tollefson. He served as an assistant guide to the famous duo for many years.

Our headquarters, at the time, was the Olga Bay Cannery. It was built in the late 1870s or early '80s and operated up until 1892 when they closed it down. Bill and Morris moved from Red River Beach over to the cannery and became watchmen just before the war [World War II]. They remained on as watchmen but they had permission to conduct their hunts out of there. Everything was old, no doubt about that, but it made a good hunting headquarters. We had running water from about mid-May through the summer until freeze-up. After that, we had to pack water from a creek. There were lots of shrimp and king crab in the bay. By the time I got there, the salmon were just about gone. They all went in a can somewhere.

It was just a great time to be on Kodiak. Any place you'd want to go ... you'd be by yourself. We had three cabins, one at Red River, one at Fraser, and one at Karluk. A few years later, we built one on the Dog Salmon River. All the cabins were completely equipped with woodstoves, bunks, sleeping bags, and food. We would re-supply them with canned goods on the last hunt we made there in the fall. We'd also cut a bunch of alder for firewood and haul it inside to dry.

At that time, we got a lot of snow in the winter. Lots of ice on the lakes. Ice didn't go out until the middle of May. Whatever cabin we selected for the April hunt, we had to snowshoe in there. That would make it hard to carry a heavy load. Hauling the supplies in during the fall made it much easier. In April, all you had to do was open the door and spend about an hour carrying out all the dried alder firewood we cut the previous fall. The only food you had to carry with you was a little bread, eggs, bacon, some meat, a little fresh stuff. Everything else was there.

A true Alaskan, Daryl found his favorite time of year in Kodiak was autumn.

Some of the most fun hunts were in September, regardless of the white sox. Most of the bears we would take would be right at dark. Sometimes, it was so darn dark you'd have to sneak around and get the bear silhouetted against the water in the lake. You were pretty much shooting at an outline but you'd catch them when they'd go out to catch a fish. They would be off shore 30 feet or so. So it was "close work," but it was really effective.

On the Dog Salmon, there are a bunch of sloughs where the salmon spawn; it's tidal influenced. In September, Morris and I would row from the cabin and put the boat at the mouth of the creek and slip up one of these sloughs. The strategy was to just sit and wait. Make sure you got the wind in your favor. Pretty soon, something would either step out of the grass on the other side of the slough or you could hear them coming up the slough, walking or catching a fish. It wasn't uncommon what showed up wasn't what you were looking for. Sometimes, three or four of them in a bunch! When you did kill a bear, you'd end up skinning it by flashlight. Usually the hunter would hold the flashlight. Anytime the fish splashed, you'd be working in the dark because the hunter would get nervous and the light would be shining out in the brush looking for bears.

Alaska's wilderness is not always a comfortable place. Heavy packs, long hikes, and insect scourges are everyday occurrences. One of the most physically-demanding aspects of hunting huge brown bears is packing out the hide. Daryl was ideally suited for the task.

In the springtime, a bear hide would weigh maybe 100 pounds, depending how much meat you left on it. Fall time, same-sized bear, maybe 120 to 125 pounds. That's a good-sized load, but in those years, I was the perfect packer. I wore a size 42 shirt and #2 hat. All I did was put it on and go! That kind of stamina is long gone. I like to say I've replaced it with knowledge!

Although the guides lived in an area surrounded by large bears, they rarely experienced any problems. However, there were a few harrowing incidents.

I'm not sure why the bears down there are not aggressive towards humans, whereas in other parts of the state, people have more concerns and fears of being attacked. Don't have a clue. All I can go by is personal experience. I never had a bear I really thought was going to do me harm, although there was one aggressive bear at the upper end of Karluk Lake.

Several of my co-workers were up there counting fish. They walked right into a sow. She just took one look at them and here she come. One guy knew he wasn't going to make it so he shimmied up this willow tree. But those willows along Canyon Creek aren't all that tall. He said he was all hunched up at the top, just like a cluster of grapes. She'd stand up on her hind feet and she just couldn't quite reach the bottom of his hip boots. She'd drop down and pace around. For whatever reason, she left him up the tree. Maybe she figured he wasn't going anywhere. She took off downstream again and found the second fellow.

He took off running and she was right after him. He saw he wasn't going to make it to the boat. He came to this bend in the creek and there's a pretty big hole there. He just bailed off and jumped clean out to the middle of this pool. He was standing in water up to his armpits and looking up at the bank and she was just standing there looking at him. Finally she just turned around and walked back up to the tree where the first guy was and fiddled around with him for about ten minutes and then turned and went upstream with her cubs and turned into the brush maybe 50 yards away.

The guy up in the tree waited a long time until he figured she was gone. He started sliding down the tree. When he put his feet down and here she comes out of the brush again. She kept him up there about 30 minutes that time. Finally, she wandered off again. He saw her quite a ways up in the brush with the kids, and they were leaving.

In the summer time (after spring hunting season was over), any place we went, we walked. I don't recall anybody ever carrying a rifle. Every once in a while you'd run into a bear. Never did have any problems. The only person in our camp, that ever got tore up was Joe Want. He'd have been about 17 years old at the time. He had been up behind the cannery in a little valley checking some otter traps. This was in November. He was coming back to camp. It was after dark and he was walking along the creek and he walked right into a sow that had two or three cubs. She took after him and he saw he wasn't going to get away, so he dove down in the niggerheads and pulled his pack-board up over his head.

She took a few bites out of the pack-board. One of the bites she took, she got the skin on the back of his arm. When she chomped down, she kind of ripped the hide around a little bit. I can still see Joe when he come into the cannery that night. His eyes were about the size of golf balls! We washed him up and put a bandage on him. It was kind of a minor item. Well, it was minor, as long as it was his arm!

Anti-hunters are one of Darrell's pet peeves. Criticizing responsible hunters and guides gets his goat.

One of the things that bothers me is bear viewing. Tourists from these large tour groups (which have become a plague in this country) want "barnyard bears" to look at. They don't want to look at wild bears, they want to look at domesticated bears. A lot of times I have been reviled for hunting bears. The thing that really torques me off is when they say if I just watched the bears, I wouldn't want to hunt them.

Well, I've spent more hours, days, and months watching bears when I was hunting than most of these so-called wildlife viewers will do in their lifetime. The largest percentage of hunting is looking and trying to find bears. When you do find bears, you try to determine what you are looking at. Out of all the bears you see, you try to pick a good one for the hunter. I spent hours every day doing that. To be accused of not watching bears, hell, I watch them just for the fun of it! A lot of times, a bear might not be one you'd want to go after but it might be doing something interesting so you'd watch it for hours. But to say me or any other guide is not a watcher of wildlife, well, it's just not true.

Farmen with a brown bear.

NORM SUTLIFF
Kodiak, AK

Norm Sutliff was raised on a farm in the Adirondack Mountains of northern New York State during the Depression.

We raised whatever we ate because there wasn't any money to buy anything in those days. I had to put meat on the table, so I became a hunter and a fisherman when I was just a young fellow. I loved the great outdoors.

He joined the Merchant Marine shortly after high school. When he left that occupation a couple years later, Norm headed to Alaska and wound up in Kodiak.

I drove across the United States in an old Ford and sold it in Seattle. I came to Alaska on an Alaska Steamship boat in steerage. When I got to Kodiak, it was the most beautiful day and the country was so green. I threw my seabag down on the dock and said, "This is where I'm going to stay. I'm through traveling."

A boat needed a cook. I went down and threw my gear on the deck.

The skipper said, "Where do you think you're going?"

I said, "I'm your new cook."

He asked, "Can you cook?"

I said, "I am without a doubt the best cook in the Territory of Alaska."

He said, "OK. There's your stateroom."

He never asked my name, social security number, where I was from, or how much money I expected to get. That's how I got my first job.

I stayed on that boat all summer. Every day was an adventure. We would anchor up in a different bay every night. In those days, you couldn't get fresh eggs. The supply boat would come in only once a month. Uganik Island is rocky and seagulls lay their eggs on the cliffs. I hung over the edge of the cliff on a rope and filled a basket with seagull eggs. We also ate clams and seal liver once or twice a week.

There were lots of clams in those days. The sea otters have since cleaned out the clams. The first year or two I was here, you just didn't see any sea otters. About three years later, I saw one on the north end of the Island. They started getting thicker and thicker. After about 20 years, they were so thick they would form rafts 15 feet square of solid sea otters. Killer whales will swim around a group of sea otter and get them all in a bunch. Then, one of the whales will come up through the middle with his mouth open. He gets quite a few of them.

In Alaska, there's sometimes conflict between domesticated animals and local wildlife. Norm saw firsthand how Kodiak's developing cattle industry served as a magnet for the Island's brown bears. The giant bears became a lifelong focus for this dedicated outdoorsman.

Two or three ranchers started raising cattle on Kodiak. They found out pretty quickly you couldn't raise cattle and brown bear on the same range. The bears would kill about ten percent of the herd every year. My role was hunting bear with dogs. When the dogs would come across a bear track, they'd start trailing. The dogs would bite the bear on the hind leg. He'd stop and fight and then he'd try to get away and then he would stop and fight. Many times the bear would head for steep country. A bear can go where a dog can't go. We got maybe one bear out of three.

On the 4th of July in 1939, Charlie Madsen called a meeting. He was the dean of guides. He could see that Kodiak Island was ideal habitat for the brown bear. He knew that homesteading would become a conflict. We drew a line across Kodiak Island. The south end is for bears and the north end is for people. Everyone was happy with that. As time went on, the Feds kinda forgot that agreement and objected to the ranchers shooting bears. They have picked on those ranchers ever since.

Norm was a devoted hunter and fisherman. He fed his family from Kodiak's bounty.

One year, I had a small boat with an outboard motor. My wife and I went out for halibut. In those days we used a hand line. She caught one weighing about 80 pounds. It was so big I didn't dare get it in the boat. I finally shot him. We ate halibut all winter long. My family also lived on venison. Every fall I would go deer hunting and get three, four, five deer and put them in our deep freeze. I never went deer hunting without my wife.

The same with fishing. I got a pilot's license in 1957 and my hobby was fishing rainbow trout on Afognak Island. We could just hop from one lake to another and fish trout all day in different spots.

One time, we stayed in a cabin at Paul's Lake. In the middle of the night, the whole cabin was shaking. The wife says, "What do you think that is?" I said, "I got a pretty good idea." I grabbed my rifle and jumped out the front door. Sure enough there was a bear stood up on its hind legs about 10 feet from me. When a bear is that close, you can't take a chance 'cause that bear could get ya in one swap. So I shot that bear.

Another time, my wife and I were at that same cabin on Afognak. There was a pool where bears came. I walked down to the edge of the stream. A bear walked out of brush on the other side. I just froze ... nothing else to do. Instead of going back the way he come, he came my way. That bear came so close that I could have put my hand on him. He never paid any attention to me. I backed up very cautiously and went back to the cabin.

One spring the banker and I went clam digging at low tide. I always carried my rifle. The banker had a fancy Weatherby with a super scope on it. A bear busted out of the brush, coming like a freight train. My partner shot and might have killed a dozen clams. The rocks and water flew, but the bear kept coming. The bear was so close when I shot that I just turned a little bit and he went right past me. The one shot killed him.

Another time, the same fellow and I were hunting bear on Afognak. It was March and the mountains was covered with snow. We could see bear tracks up on the mountain. We decided to go take a look. Unbeknownst to us, there was a little dip about half way up the mountain. A bear was asleep right there. As we came over the rim, he charged us. Within a matter of seconds he was on top of us. My partner shot and the snow flew and the bear kept coming. I shot once and killed him. Those are the only two bears I can think of that ever charged me.

Local residents worked together with agency personnel to create one of the most productive salmon runs on the Island.

Two years before we became a state, the government sent over a biologist to get acquainted. He recognized that the Frazer River could be a great salmon stream except for some falls at the bottom of the lake. The fish couldn't get up to the lake. His idea was to put in a fish ladder. He talked one of the local pilots into flying some red salmon from Red River into Frazer Lake. It was just a five minute flight. They made special floats for the airplane. They put salmon in the floats, flew them over, and let them go.

Those salmon didn't like Frazer Lake. They went down the river and swam back to the Red River where we caught them. We put a little fence across so they couldn't get out and flew in another batch. They stayed and spawned. Two years later they came back, but he didn't have the fish ladder in, yet. I built a box the length of a fish. We'd fill it with water and two or three fish and run up to the falls and let them go. We back-packed the first run of red salmon up through them falls. Then the biologist was able to convince the powers-that-be to put in a fish ladder. It was a huge success.

Norm has interacted with many agency personnel over the years. He can't forget the good ones.

Will Troyer was the Refuge Manager here for many years. Instead of sitting in an office, he was outdoors all the time. He knew what was going on and everyone was crazy about him.

Elk weren't native to Afognak Island. They were imported and released. Hunting was prohibited for years until the herd built up. I went elk hunting the first year it was open. It was illegal to shoot a spike, but I hadn't read the regulations carefully. Five or six of us went hunting, and we each got an elk. About three or four of them were spikes. We threw all the horns in the skiff. Will Troyer come aboard and had coffee. A couple years later, he and I were discussing that trip.

I said, "Boy, those spikes tasted good."

He said, "What do you mean spikes?"

I said, "Pretty near half of those elk in that skiff was spikes."

He said, "Did you know it was against the law?"

I said, "Hell no, I didn't know it was against the law."

It was two or three years later, so he just overlooked it.

Norm served on the State's Guide Board for several years in the 1960s. He appreciated the commitment of prospective guides who traveled from the far corners of the State to obtain a license.

I enjoyed every minute of it and met some wonderful people. They used to call me 'No Horse**** Sutliff' 'cause I'd speak up and stick to my guns. Guides and hunters came long distances via skiff or dog team to those meetings. Some of them couldn't speak English. I always looked after their interest.

We conducted exams for new guides. One time in Nome, a couple Eskimos applied for a license. A Board member asked one of them how he dealt with hypothermia.

The Eskimo said, "I don't know what you're talking about." He never heard of it.

I asked, "What do you do when your feet get wet?"

He said, "Eskimo don't get his feet wet."

I passed him 'cause he was telling it straight. In their culture, they're taught to be careful and avoid getting their feet wet.

We also tested their knowledge of caring for meat and hides. I asked one of those guys how to flesh a polar bear. He said, "That's women's work." In their culture, the woman is the one who handles hides. I passed him, too.

Norm explains one of the most appealing features of life in Alaska prior to statehood.

It was a great country back when I first got here. In those days, we really understood what freedom was. You didn't have the feds or the state or the borough to make laws. You could get up in the morning and go any direction you wanted and do whatever you wanted. Today we have restrictions and laws and rules and regulations. We really knew what freedom was in those days. I wouldn't change my life here for anything.

{NORM SUTLIFF PASSED AWAY IN 2008}

JOHN NICHOLSON
Dillingham, AK

John Nicholson was born at a salmon cannery in Clark's Point, on Bristol Bay, in 1906. The family later moved to the Ekuk cannery, a couple of miles away.

We lived there for seven years. My parents sent me to school in Nushyak. I stayed with my grandma. Then we lived at a cannery in Kanulik for a while. That's an abandoned village now. The cannery closed because it got too shallow. In the fall of 1925, my dad took a job as a watchman in old Dillingham, which is called Kanakanak now.

There were a lot of Natives living in Dillingham before 1919, but the Spanish influenza killed many people. The disease hit the States in 1918. When the cannery people came up the next summer, they brought it with them. It wiped out most of the Native elders. There were a lot of children without parents around here, so they started an orphanage in old Dillingham.

Nicholson was a dedicated trapper from an early age, targeting primarily beaver and fox, using techniques he learned from local Natives.

I've been trapping all my life. I was 12 years old when I first started to trap. I learned from a Yupik. I was pretty friendly with the Yupik people. I trapped the way he trapped.

I used a dog team for transportation on the trapline. I had nine dogs in my team. I cooked salmon for my dogs. They were big husky dogs that could run for miles every day on the trapline.

Back in the olden days, white people would go up the Nushagak River to trap. Beaver were high-priced then. Back in the 1920s, a big blanket beaver was worth $100. Some trappers made a living just by trapping beaver.

Beaver trapping was closed for a good many years. They finally opened it in 1927. I went 30 miles upriver with an Eskimo boy and started beaver trapping. I would pitch a 10 x 12 tent. The limit was 20 beaver.

Upriver the beaver taste really "sprucey," but my wife knew how to cook it. She soaked them in salt water overnight. When she cooked the beaver they don't smell or taste like spruce.

Fox have a good nose. They can smell the steel of a trap. Some fox are pretty smart. They'll circle a set to check it out before they go in. I use bait at the main set. In winter-time, the wind generally comes from a northerly direction and fox always go against the wind, so I put the bait on the north side of the trap. I set a "blind" trap about four or five feet away from the main trap. When they circle around the main trap, they forget about that blind set. While he's eating the bait, he gets caught in the trap. That's how I trick those smart ones.

I used to average 15 or 20 red fox every winter. At that time, red fox skins weren't too valuable ... maybe $20. A few years afterwards, I got $150 for a nice red fox. One winter I caught a couple cross foxes. Cross foxes were more valuable.

There was a local furbuyer in Dillingham. He bought a lot of my fur. After he passed away, I sold my fur to buyers that came in from Anchorage. The main one was Kosloskey. He treated everybody fair. I took him up the Nushagak River by boat to buy beavers. We went up almost 100 miles and come down with 800 beavers in the boat.

While John fished and trap for money, his hunting skills were put to one use – to feed his family.

There used to be a lot of ptarmigan all over. When I would leave my house, I would see ptarmigan all the way upriver and never be out of sight of them. They were by the thousands … millions! When there's a lot of snow, the ptarmigan would come down towards Dillingham. More than 500 in a flock in the olden days. Now, there's a few but the flocks are small. Ravens eat ptarmigan eggs. My belief is the ptarmigan will be extinct if they don't get rid of the ravens.

Ducks and geese come in April. We used to hunt them for meat in the olden days. We only had reindeer meat and ptarmigan in the winter until the ducks and geese came back in the spring. We're not supposed to hunt ducks in the spring, but that was our custom in the olden days.

When I was young, there were no moose around here. I had to go upriver a 100 miles or so. Now, there's moose all over.

John spent his life as a commercial fisherman in Bristol Bay. He began fishing at age 12 and continued for 65 years. He took great pride in his hard work and success.

When I was a kid, my Dad told me there were millions and millions of salmon. You'd see spawning salmon up Wood River Lakes over a foot deep. Now, there are no more big runs. I call them big schools, that's all! I tell Fish and Game people they have a lot of learn about salmon. My belief is nobody knows much about salmon … not even me!

There are a lot of predators on salmon. They blame belugas for eating up young salmon. But there's the seals, fish, ducks, and a lot of marine life that are eating up the young salmon, too. And there's the "draggers" out there. They'll drag anything in their nets. There's a lot of reasons we have less salmon. Salmon got too many enemies, as I see it.

There are a lot of belugas around. In the olden days, there were a lot of Natives that liked to hunt belugas and seals. The young people here in Dillingham don't seem to go out for belugas like they used to. We used to have fish by the millions. Now, if they don't get rid of some of the predators, it's gonna be years and years before the salmon run builds up.

I was one of the first set-netters. When they opened the season, I was 12 years old. My dad helped me with my first site on the beach at Ekuk. He also bought me a little skiff. When the weather was fine, I rowed the fish to the cannery. I was a big husky boy. I also had my five dogs to pull a two-wheeled fish cart to the cannery when the weather wasn't so good. I delivered fish both ways -- fine weather by boat and rough weather by dog team.

I set-netted until I was 15 years old. Then, Alaska Packers gave me a sailboat. After I picked my set net, I went out gill-netting with the sailboat. When we used sailboats, we fished six days per week.

The cannery had a lot of sailboats before power boats became available. Two men to a boat … the captain and boat puller. The boat puller rowed the boat and pulled up the sail. The captain threw the net out. In fine weather, the sailboat will hold 1,800 fish. When it was a little choppy, I would have 1,200 to 1,500 fish in a boat. The canneries hired us to fish in their boats and we got paid so much per fish. I was getting 5 cents for a whole salmon.

We generally threw the net out and then went to sleep. We used the sail as a tent and reindeer skins for mattress and blankets. We were young and tough and we didn't mind it. Sleep with our clothes on, kick our rubber boots off. If big storms came up when we were fishing out of the sailboat, we'd go anchor on the sheltered side of the river. Then wait until the wind died down a little bit. Usually, that was no more than half a day.

I was against the use of power boats. The Superintendent at the Ekuk cannery was against the power boat. The fisherman voted for the power boat and they got it. When they started using power boats, the price of salmon went up over $2 a pound. Now, it's dropped down to 20 cents a pound. Hardly worth going fishing anymore with powerboats. Gasoline is a high price now. Got to catch a lot of fish to make any money. A lot of the fisherman wind up in the hole. I still tell fisherman, "Go back to the sailboat. You'll make money." Wind power is cheap.

I still fish and haul the fish up from the beach. I eat a lot of dry fish in the wintertime.

John has been part of the subsistence debate for decades. He has a simple solution to the controversy.

My belief on subsistence is when there is a lot of game around, everybody should be able to hunt. When there's not a lot of game, people in the villages should be allowed to hunt for a little meat if they are hard up. That could be regulated very easily. But not if people start voting on it. Naturally everybody wants to hunt and eat game.

I'm afraid it will wind up with a federal takeover. That's bad for Alaska. We should do what WE want to do. Other states have their own way. Why can't Alaska have its own way? They have been arguing for years and nobody seems to agree. I think it's simple. Do it the old way. Let everybody hunt and fish. When there's not much game around, they could regulate it.

John was born in Alaska when it was still a territory. Unlike many residents, he wasn't for a fan of statehood.

Most people liked it when the territory became a state, but I think I had more freedom when Alaska was a territory. After statehood, the legislature passed a lot of laws that I don't agree with.

I was born here and used to be proud of Alaska. I used to talk about "Alaska, my country." But I don't brag about Alaska any more. I blame Juneau and the legislature. I figure most of those guys are Outsiders and they get elected because they are better talkers than the residents. Those people move up here from the States and after a few years, they go back to the States. I don't think they care too much for this state. There's a few legislators born in Alaska, but they get out-talked. That's my belief.

Fishing and trapping constituted the focus of John Nicholson's entire life. He speaks with candor of an era when life was both simple and hard.

I was born and raised here in Alaska and want to stick to it. I'm 96 years old [in 2002]; the oldest man in Dillingham. I'm in pretty good shape. I feel young yet.

I've been hunting and fishing and trapping all my life. I trapped last winter and caught five beavers and an otter. Nowadays, I lose money trapping. Gasoline is high when I go out with the snow-go. It don't hardly pay.

I like to go ptarmigan hunting if there's any around. I shot five ptarmigan the other day; four of them with one shot. I still go snow-machining, although I was leery of them for years after they first came out. I go out in the woods. I burn wood. I do everything young people do.

It's been a good and active life for me. I worked plenty. I eat a lot of wild salmon, that's why I lived this long.

{JOHN NICHOLSON PASSED AWAY IN 2003}

Kenai Peninsula

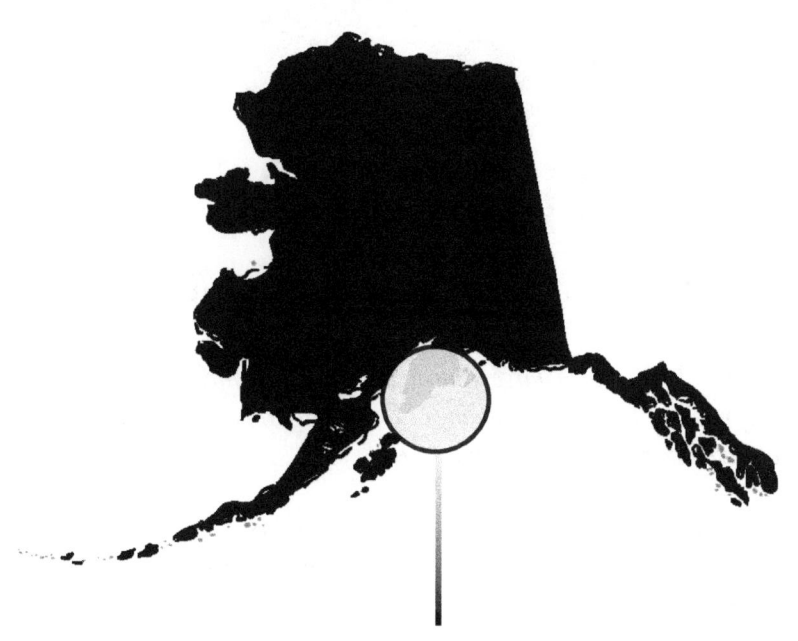

Area of detail

Cooper Landing, Soldotna, Homer

WILL TROYER

Cooper Landing, AK

Will Troyer was born into a large Amish family which farmed in Indiana during the Great Depression. He had six siblings. The family raised everything they ate. He developed an interest in wildlife from a very early age.

We considered the wildlife on the farm to be a "crop" similar to hay or livestock. That's how I got into hunting and fishing. My mother encouraged me to get a couple cotton-tail rabbits for the larder. That was a change of diet, instead of fried chicken and beef.

My second-grade teacher got me interested in birds. In the spring of the year, she'd ask, "Who saw the first robin?" If you were first, she'd write your name on the blackboard. She made a game out of it. I became very interested in birds and wildlife. In those days, Arm & Hammer Baking Soda had an ad in all the farm magazines, offering colored bird cards. Those were the only bird identification materials we had for many years.

When I was 11 years old, my mother told me about a bird book in one of the stores. It cost $3.95. I saved my pennies and eventually bought it. She wrote my name and the date inside. It was 1936, when I was 11 years old. Within a year, I knew every bird in Indiana. I've still got that book.

My oldest brother and I became avid hunters. We started at an early age. The first time I can remember going hunting, I was probably six or seven years old. We had a big snow, probably 12 inches. I noticed a cottontail rabbit track. I followed it through the cornfield and orchard. Sure enough, I finally saw it sitting there. I ran back to the house and told my dad, "Get your shotgun. We've got a cottontail out here." He was just about to shoot it when he decided to save the cost of a three-penny shell. He took the shell out and hit the rabbit in the head with it. I claimed that as "my" rabbit and took it to my mother. She fried it up for supper.

Will went to college in Oregon and received a degree in wildlife management. That led to a long and distinguished career as a wildlife biologist.

I came to Alaska in 1951 and have been here ever since. I was sent to Yakutat as a weir watchmen on the Situk River. As a young college kid and a farm boy from the Midwest, I was in heaven. After we got the weir in, there were steelhead in the river. So I fished steelhead pretty hard. Then the king salmon started. Man, I fished myself to death on the kings. Then the silvers started. It was really good.

When I arrived, the Fish & Wildlife Service had three or four biologists, seven or eight predator control men (that was the second largest branch), and probably 25 enforcement guys. The first three years in Alaska, I primarily worked on protection assignments in Southeastern. We were doing wildlife patrols and checking deer hunters. We also worked on the duck flats and I got to do a lot of hunting on my own.

Life on the Refuge was hardly calm. Troyer first made a name for himself as the manager of the Kodiak Wildlife Refuge. There were battles between wildlife managers, cattle ranchers, bear guides, and businessmen over bear management.

Brown bears were very unpopular. The ranchers in Kodiak were trying to get a cattle industry going. The Chamber of Commerce types in Kodiak thought the bears were killing too many cattle and hindering the project. The fisherman thought the bears were competing with them for salmon. Basically, people didn't think much of bears and they were shooting them at every opportunity. There was some experimental work, trying to use electric fences to keep them out of salmon streams. It worked to a certain degree.

Early in his tenure, he recognized the necessity of gathering basic biological information on the large brown bears which inhabit the Island. The first capture efforts were less than smooth, but the process evolved in later years.

I saw the need for scientific studies. In order to get the necessary information, I felt that we had to get ear tags in the bears. Up 'til that time, nobody had ever captured one. Some of the black bear biologists in the states were using steel traps to catch bears. Then they'd put a bucket of ether over its head and knock it out. I figured I could do that with brown bear. When I told everybody that I was going to trap bears, they laughed at me. I had a dozen traps. They weren't real big, as I recall. I figured a big bear would never get his foot in there, but I didn't want to catch the big ones. The first year, I caught eight bears; all sub-adults that weighed 200 to 300 pounds. We had a team of three guys. Two would throw ropes over the bear's head and pull in opposite directions. The third guy (usually me) would have a bucket with a bunch of cotton in it. I'd pour some ether in the bucket, slip it over the bear's head, and knock them out.

The next year, the black bear biologists came up with a new drug called succinylcholine. It knocked them out for a maximum five minutes. You still had to hog-tie them and give them some sodium pentabarbital to put them to sleep, but it was a LOT better than a bucket of ether. We had a syringe on the end of a 12-foot aluminum pole. When we had a bear in the trap, one person would get their attention and another person would slip behind them and jab them with the syringe. It would take them a few minutes to go down and they would only stay out for a few minutes. We would rush in and hog-tie them and give them the other drug. It would take at least 20 minutes to put them to sleep. Once they were asleep, they were down for an hour or two. With the new drugs, I managed to tag and release 30 bears that summer. Over the years, we did about 200 bears that same way. We got the technique down! Now, most of the bears are darted from the air. I did all my bear work on the ground.

Studies of the captured bears produced new info regarding many aspects of their biology and behavior.

When I first started this bear work, it was before radio collars were available. We tattooed their lips and put ear tags in them. Then we did some experimental work with colored collars. We were able to identify quite a few bears at close range. We did counts of the collared bears vs. the non-collared. We knew how many were in the drainage and that would give us an idea what the total population was. We took weights and measurements to help determine growth rates. Prior to that, nobody knew how long it took for a big boar to grow up. We learned quite a bit about movements. We got to know the size of the population in some of the prime bear habitat. We came up with a population estimate of around 2,500 bears. A few years ago, with all this modern technology, they came up with an estimate within 100 bears of what we had estimated back then.

Local bear hunting guides earned their knowledge the hard way. Will credits the guides for sharing their vast knowledge with him.

When I first got to Kodiak, there were eight or nine guys who made a living guiding bear hunters. The guides advertised in "Field & Stream." If you go back to the old magazines, you can see their ads. They're pretty interesting. The guides had been doing it for years and had a lot of knowledge. I went on a hunt with one of them. I quizzed him on bear behavior and a lot of other things. I learned a lot about bears by going with them.

I encouraged the guiding because it helped off-set the objections we had from the cattle industry. We had guides charging $1,000 per hunt and making a lot of money. The Chamber of Commerce and the people in Kodiak started seeing that, too. I started dragging the guides into some of the Chamber meetings so they could tell their side of the situation. It counteracted the bad press the bears had gotten from the fishermen and cattle industry. I went to the guides when I wanted support for the bears. The guides were somewhat organized and that was my only support for the bears and refuge at that time. That's one of the smartest things I ever did.

Many years later, I worked seven seasons with a bear-viewing outfit. It was great to sit there day after day, eyeball to eyeball, really close to bears. I learned more about bears doing that than I did when I was a biologist. I didn't have the time as a biologist to sit there and observe and have the interactions with them. I should have done that earlier in my career instead of later.

Will became Refuge Manager on the Kenai in 1963. In this new position, he developed the canoe systems on the northern half of the Peninsula. Once again, Will's work ethic led to the success of the project.

That was my pet project. Other people had talked about it, but nobody was doing anything. We just started cutting trails. A couple times a week, I'd take one of the guys in my Super Cub and we'd cut another portage. We did that all winter long. By the next spring, we had a small part of the system in place.

There are two areas -- Swanson River and Swan Lake. The first loop was pretty straight-forward. It was completed in 1964. The first spring after we completed that first loop, I got in a canoe and went around it one weekend. I was convinced we had something pretty good. When I put the Swanson River loop in, we sampled all those lakes to find out which ones had fish. We selected a route so we'd hit as many fishing lakes as possible.

I did it for two reasons. One was to build up the recreation and the other was that the oil people wanted to put oil wells everywhere on the Kenai at that time. I thought that shouldn't be allowed. The canoe systems helped us. They put a value on the refuge. I still go out into the canoe system every year. It's really fine fly-fishing. The Kenai River might be covered with people trying to catch a king salmon, but you can go out to the canoe system and get a lake to yourself. It's a really high quality type of recreation.

Big game was an important source of protein when Will was raising a family. He now avidly pursues grouse and ptarmigan with a pointing dog. Like all hunters, Will has evolved. As a mature hunter, he can now appreciate his time in the field, regardless of the level of harvest.

One of my most memorable hunts was the first time I ever went sheep hunting. Jack Lentfer and I went up in the Chugach Mountains. It took us a couple days to hike into this valley. After three or four days, we finally spotted some sheep up on a big snow field. We had to go around behind them, but they detected us. I'll never forget that scene. Nine great big rams (all full curl) were walking over an ice field towards a glacier. We thought we really messed up. We happened to notice one big old ram and one small one way up above, separated from the others. We split up. Jack went up high and I went down low. I was sneaking up on these last rams and just set my rifle on a stone to take a shot when "BOOM." Jack shot and mine jumped up. I picked out the biggest one and got it. I thought it was a pretty nice ram. It was 42 inches on one side and broomed on the other. I dressed it out and hauled it back to our little bivouac camp. Jack didn't show up for hours. Finally, here he comes. I was pretty proud of my ram until he threw his horns down. I forget the dimensions but it was third in the Boone & Crockett book. We got a fire started and started roasting ribs. We had been eating dried food for a couple of days, so those ribs tasted great. It took us three or four days to get out. Our packs weighed 100 pounds apiece. It was a great experience. It was a long walk, but we were in there by ourselves. We went back three or four years in a row.

Years ago, I started hunting moose with a friend. Whoever shot the first moose, the other guy would help pack it out. When that was done, the second guy would hunt. When he got his animal, he called the first guy. We did that for probably 20 years. Moose was a serious thing. That meat was very important to our families. After the kids started leaving, we cut back and would take one between us.

I'll take deer hunting over any other species. I call deer a lot. I learned that skill in Southeast. The Natives call deer down there by blowing through a blade of grass. Everybody else just whittled their own whistle. I got pretty good at it. It's a good experience to be able to call a deer in, especially on Kodiak. A lot of times I have called a deer from pretty high up on the mountain down to a much lower elevation. It saved me a lot of work. The does often come running full bore, but the bucks usually come sneaking in. Once in a while, you do have a buck that comes running in. Out of all the deer I have killed, I suspect that over half have come in to the call.

I've turned into a very avid bird hunter, with the help of a dog. When I was a kid, I had a beagle to hunt rabbits. In 1954, I got my first lab, and had Labs until 1968 when I got a pointing dog. I was one of the earliest people to use a pointing dog. Now I have become such an avid bird hunter I don't have time for anything else. Most people shoot grouse along the roads. If you start hunting grouse in the woods and you make up your mind you are only going to shoot birds on the wing, that's one of the meanest targets there is!

The young boy infatuated with birds and animals was able to fulfill his dream of a life in the outdoors studying and hunting the wildlife he loves. He's thought a lot about the motivations for hunting, and has refined his personal philosophy.

You hear Natives say how they are tied to the land and wildlife. I'm the same way. I was brought up that way. It's very important for me to fill my freezer and eat the game I harvested. Not only with wild meat but with fish and berries. It's a good satisfying feeling. Ever since I've been up here, I always filled our freezer. I spent three years in Wrangell and Juneau, where I concentrated on deer and ducks and fish. I was on Kodiak for eight years. There it was mainly deer, elk, waterfowl, ptarmigan, and salmon.

My hunting has changed over the years. My major interest used to be big game. I've learned that I don't really like to kill big game unless I utilize it all myself. In recent years, with my kids gone, we don't need as much meat. I hunt with a friend over on Kodiak. I get two or three deer and that will last us for a couple years.

The longer I've been hunting, the more I like to revert to primitive hunting. I really think the sportsmen kind of wrecked it when they got too mechanized. I'm not against a guy using a four-wheeler to go back in somewhere, but I think we ought to confine ourselves to certain areas instead of running all over. We lost something when we started relying on new technology. It gives us a bad reputation. We would have a better reputation if we had a little more physical effort to it rather than all those modern devices.

My philosophy on hunting has changed. As you get older, you look at things differently. The longer I hunt, the more important it is to me just to be in the field and not worry about how much game I get. I used to worry about that. If the bag limit was 20 ptarmigan, I'd get 20 ptarmigan. Now, it's more important to have a good time and a good outdoor experience. The shooting is only part of it.

Looking back, I had a great career. It was a good time to come up here. I know I couldn't get away with stuff now like I did back then. When I wanted to do something, I just did it. I didn't ask Washington for approval. In a way, my hunting and fishing and work all flowed together. In those days, we were working with the animals instead of sitting behind a computer. It was similar to when you were hunting. Whether you're a hunter or a biologist, one of the factors in success is the amount of time you spend in the field.

A young Troyer holding a fresh catch.

LYLE GARNER
Soldotna, AK

Lyle Garner has lived and worked many places throughout Alaska, from the frozen Interior to the dangerous waters of the Bering Sea. It was a tough and dangerous life.

We fished the Bering Sea for crab. I didn't like that country up there so good. Rough ... bad weather. When you're fishing in that district, you figure you'll lose three to five percent of the guys you start the year with. Somebody goes. After awhile you had all new guys! None of the old timers were there. Most of my friends died fishing. That's the second roughest water in the world. I got lucky and lived through all of it. I figured the Lord was on my side. He gave me lots of chances.

Back in the 1950s, Alaska was a rough and tumble place. Men who spent months in the Bush found many temptations when they came to town.

I was fighting a dude one time in front of the old Shanty Bar. He was a big man. We'd been fighting for some time and some woman called the police. Here come the U.S. Marshall with a deputy. She says, "Aren't you going to stop that!" He says, "No I ain't gonna stop it. It's a good fight! I'm gonna watch it." I never will forget that.

Pretty soon that big dude I was fighting with says, "You tired of this?" I says, "Yeah." He says, "Me too. Let's go get drunk." So we did. Nobody was really mad at each other. We just settled our differences.

The Fur Rendezvous in Anchorage is now largely a collection of social and sporting events. Prior to Statehood, the "Rondy" was an opportunity for trappers and furbuyers to gather and transact business.

We had the Rendezvous in Anchorage. What I'm talking about back then isn't the Rendezvous they have now. The trapping season closed at the end of February, so we all came into town the first week of March to sell our furs. We'd go to the Federal Building on Fourth Avenue. In the back, there was a jail. In front, all the state offices, and on the left side in the back was the Game Commission. The Game Commission had a big room and we'd bring all of our furs in there and pile them on the floor. The Game Commission would go through and tag what they wanted to tag. The buyers would walk through and bid so much on lynx, so much on wolverine, and so much on beaver. Whoever bid the most, got the furs. That was how it came to be called the Fur Rendezvous.

After the furs were sold, it was time for a drink. Bob Hope came through town one year. He's riding in an open top limousine and he's talking to everybody up and down Fourth Avenue. Old Bob Hope says, "Geez, this Fourth Avenue is the longest bar in the world!" Everybody had a gun on their hip. Anchorage was the wildest town you'd ever imagine in them days.

Garner trapped on Kodiak Islamd for a number of years. He often skinned animals at the site where they were caught, rather than carry the entire carcass back to his cabin. One ingenious bear learned Lyle's habit and took advantage of a free lunch.

When you got a bear on a trapline, it's either a good one or a bad one. I had what I called an "old man bear." Big fellow. He was the biggest bear I ever saw. He followed me for about 20 years. I would see him quite often. He'd be on the trail behind me when I skinned a beaver. I'd put the hide in my pack and leave the carcass behind. If I'd go back 30 minutes later, there ain't no beaver but lots of big bear tracks!

One time, we accidentally got 12 or 14 feet from each other. He stopped and I stopped. He slowly backed up and went the other way to get away from me. Never no hair up or never no growls, just a "woof woof," that's all the noise them big bears will make. He was never aggressive, because I was his source for easy food.

He followed me all winter long. He would never take nothing out of my cache or my traps. He was an easy one to get along with. The last year I trapped, he was still there.

During his years on Kodiak, Lyle learned a lot about the behavior of giant brown bears. He describes an incident involving his partner and a curious bear on the west side of Cook Inlet.

Back in the '50s, we dug clams commercially on Swikshak Beach on the Alaska Peninsula. There's about 40 miles of it, from Cape Douglas all the way down to Big River. It's just full of bears there. Wherever the best clams was, we built a place to stay so the bears couldn't get in. We wanted to sleep without a bear snorting on us. We built what we called a crib house. You put two logs this way and two logs this way. We went up about four foot and put visqueen over the top to keep the rain out. And a crawl hole for us to get in and out.

I had a partner by the name of Ray Demientoff. He crawled out of that hole to go to the bathroom about 3:00 or 4:00 in the morning. It was still just a little dark. He walked over to the edge of the clearing and was emptying himself out there on the sand. A bear walked up behind him and stuck its head between his legs right at his knees and went brrrrrrrrRRRRRRR right up him and raised him off the ground! Ray let out the worst scream I ever heard. He jumped right over the top of that four-foot crib house, crashed through the visqueen, and come down right on top of me. There was sand and snot all over his legs where that bear's nose came up, slobbers and all. The bear didn't hurt Ray, but it took him a couple hours to calm down.

Garner had many encounters with the large bears. Unlike most other people, he was rarely frightened by these animals.

You got good dogs and bad dogs. Why not the same with bears? They ain't all good fellows. Ain't something to hug. Just give them their room. I've had some make a false charge; come 30 feet away and slam their feet down. Snort and pop their teeth and raise all kinds of ruckus, but if they stop 30 feet away and you slowly back off, they will rarely ever follow you. They just want you to move.

You see one of those big babies coming toward you with his hair standing on end, slobbers running out of his mouth, shaking his head, popping his teeth and growling. He'll get your attention. He'll make you back up pretty good. If you break and run, you're dead. You have to keep your gun on him, too. I had one at a beaver house once and I shot a slug into the beaver house to try and make him leave. I had a bunch of traps in there and he knew I had some beavers. That's why he was there. I was looking over the barrel and the next thing I knew he was standing up close! When I shot into the beaver house, he charged. He stopped maybe 30 feet or so, went to slamming his feet down and roaring. His hair was all up. I backed slowly out of there. I went back to the boat and got the .338 magnum. Come back and he was gone. I didn't shoot him and he didn't eat the beaver either. He left after I upset him. After that, I had the big gun along in that particular area instead of a shotgun. He was a big bear too, a ten-footer. You don't mess with that type. They can kill you real quick.

Prior to Statehood, federal agencies often assigned college students to remote outposts for summer duty. Garner had minimal regard for the college kids with little (or no) experience.

One year the Park Service wanted to take everybody's guns. They didn't want us to shoot no bears. I told them, "You're not taking mine." The Parkies had a tin shack right on the beach. This young college kid had all his stuff in it. One day, a bear came along and just scattered his stuff all over the beach. So this Park Service kid come to my place because I'm the only one with a gun. He says, "Come and help me. There's a bear tearing my shack down." I says, "No. You go talk to that bear and tell him he can't do that!" I wouldn't help him a bit. Teach him a lesson. He come up here and thought if you saw a bear and just said 'hello' he'll walk on. It just don't work that way.

The Alaska Department of Fish and Game stationed "Creek Guards" at the outlet of many salmon streams. These crews were responsible for protecting the returning salmon from fishermen who would not obey boundaries.

Fish and Game had a creek watchman in Discovery Bay on Afognak Island during the 50s. He made himself a toilet by nailing a couple of two-by-fours between two trees. It was only 30 feet from his cabin but the tide come up and kept it clean! Well, he didn't realize the bears go up and down the beach, too. He's brand new at the business, he's a college kid. He left his gun at the cabin and brought himself some reading material. He was setting up there on the throne reading the funny papers. So he looked over the top of it and the bear's reading the other side!

I said, "What did you do?" He says, "What do you think I did? I just sat there and stared at him 'til he left." He runs up to the cabin, yelling at me to call the plane! He was really hollering to get out of there. The bear didn't do anything, just looked at him. I got a kick out of that.

Lyle worked hard all his life. He endured many challenges and discomforts. He now lives near the community of Soldotna on the Kenai Peninsula. Nearing 80 years of age, he recently bought a small sawmill. He harvests logs and produces lumber because ... "I hate to be idle." He can't imagine any other life.

Kodiak has always been my favorite place for trapping, hunting and fishing. The fishing there is fabulous. There's so much food there, it's easy to come by. Lots of ducks and geese. You can throw out a pot and get crab and shrimp anytime. Lots of game and you can make a living trapping. If I had a place to start young again, it would be Kodiak.

I wouldn't take a factory job anywhere. You can make a living doing that kind of stuff, but it takes a certain breed of cat to work his whole life doing the same thing over and over. I could never do that. I wanted to see a bear in my trail here and there. Have a rough ride on the ocean! A little adrenalin shaking you up. Without it, life's too humdrum. Adrenalin is part of your life. The more of it you get into, the more you like it. We were out there on the ocean sometimes, where a man in his right mind wished a chopper would come down and get him off. I have to admit, sometimes I wished I wasn't there. But if I had the chance to live my life over again, I'd do the same thing. And now, I've got all of those great memories.

JIM REARDEN
Homer, AK

Jim Rearden came to Alaska in the summer of 1947, to work for the Fish & Wildlife Service as a fishery patrol agent (aka "stream guard"). He returned several years later (following college) to develop a wildlife management curriculum at the University of Alaska in Fairbanks. Within a few years, Jim realized the academic world was "... not for me." He wanted more "adventure."

I was a student in Fish & Game Management at Oregon State. At the end of my senior year, I was accepted in the graduate school at the University of Maine. I spent two years there and graduated with a master's degree. I learned they were looking for someone to go to Fairbanks to teach wildlife management. I applied for it and to my amazement, I was given the job. I'm rather proud of the students I had at the time. They were really the cream of the crop. Most of them were veterans studying on the G.I. Bill, just as I had done.

Teaching wasn't for me. I always felt that the students were smarter than

I was and I had to work hard to stay ahead of them. From the classroom, I could look across the Tanana Flats at the Alaska Range. I'd be lecturing and wondering, "What am I doing here with all that wonderful country and all the adventures that a guy could have out there?" I ran into an old guide by the name of Frank Glaser. Frank was wonderful at telling stories. He was a sourdough the old-timers respected as a capable woodsmen. I started writing stories with Frank and sold a bunch of them. That gave me enough courage to resign my professorship. I wanted adventure and change and I got it. In retrospect, that was probably very foolish.

Jim moved his family to Homer in order to escape the harsh Interior winters and to be close to the ocean. For a couple of years, he bounced from job to job, trying to keep a roof over their heads and food on the table. Rearden's writing career also grew during this period.

At the time, the Interior climate was not as mild as it is these days. We had a lot of 50- and 60-below months. Homer had a lot to offer. I had to do whatever I could to bring in a few bucks. I worked as a carpenter in Homer and as a clerk in a trading post. I spent one summer hunting seals for the $3 bounty.

When I moved to Homer, we had a heck of a population of moose. I enjoy hunting and I've got a son who really loved to hunt. We would take a little ATV and go back up to the Caribou Hills with a wall tent, cots, and a wood stove. We would slip out of camp early each morning. Each of the kids would have their turn to shoot the animal. We'd dress him out, take care of the meat, and retrieve it with the machine. Over the years, I hauled more than 25 moose out of the Caribou Hills with that little machine and we ate every little bit of it.

I was writing all this time and developing relationships with editors. I had been struggling to keep alive. Writing is not a real high-paying job, at least it wasn't for me. "Outdoor Life" was my major market. I've written a lot of bear attack stories. That's a real popular thing, especially with "Outdoor Life." They made them too lurid and gory. I got a little bit upset and backed off on that. For 20 years, I was listed on the masthead of "Outdoor Life" as a field editor.

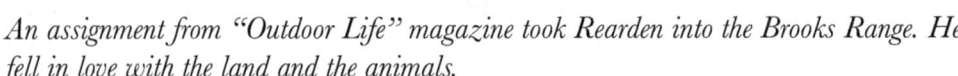

An assignment from "Outdoor Life" magazine took Rearden into the Brooks Range. He fell in love with the land and the animals.

At that time, the Brooks Range was largely unknown and un-hunted. A lot of it was unmapped. There were very few people. Only a couple guides operated in the whole Brooks Range.

The Brooks Range became my favorite place. I guided five parties up there over the years. The evening is my favorite time of day up there. It's calm. It's quiet. You can sit on the hillside with binoculars and glass the whole country. You see the moose come out, you see bears, a squirrel chatters here, a little squawk there, you see the jays flying around. It's just the quiet, calm, the peace and the beauty. It's part of hunting that is almost indescribable.

I also took a summer jaunt to the Koyukuk Valley. There was a graduate student studying the beaver population in that drainage. The local protection officer flew us up to the Huslia River. We drifted down, counting beaver and live-trapping them. We wound up at the village of Huslia. We flew to Bettles but it was going to be the next day before there would be a flight to Fairbanks. The pilot said, "Why don't you take my riverboat and go moose hunting." We got into the foothills of the Brooks Range and that country impressed me.

I also did several articles for National Geographic. I wrote one on caribou. That was a real interesting project. I flew up to Anaktuvuk Pass. I stayed at the same cabin as an old Eskimo known as Arctic John. He had killed a couple caribou in the hills and he invited me to go with him. He told stories and he sang for me. He dressed these caribou and said, "It's time for Eskimo lunch." He reached down into the gut pile, pulled out a kidney, sliced off chunks and ate them raw.

The new Alaska Department of Fish and Game hired Jim in 1959 as a Fisheries Biologist. His biggest challenge was to reverse the mismanagement that occurred under the federal system prior to statehood.

During the summer of '59, the Fish and Wildlife Service was going to manage the salmon fisheries for the last season. The new state was going to take over in 1960. The headquarters for commercial fisheries was in Homer. That summer, we flew with the Fish & Wildlife Service and followed their procedures in managing the salmon fishery. They would fly over the fishery and pick up salmon fish tickets and that was the full extent of their management program. As a result, the salmon fishery had gone to hell. In 1959, the last year of federal management, the catch in Alaska totaled 25 million salmon. The state has built this fishery back. These days if we don't get 150 or 200 million, it's an off year.

I moved up to the position of Area Biologist in 1962. The first few years of salmon management were key. The Commissioner delegated the authority to use field announcements to open and close salmon fishing seasons. This gave us the ability to stop a fishery when it was threatening good escapement AND, when there was an abundance of fish, we could allow the fisherman to take what was available. Boy, was that popular with the fisherman after all the years of federal management.

Jim instituted a new approach of open communication with the commercial fisherman in the waters surrounding the Kenai Peninsula.

I started a radio program that we called "Fisherman's Corner." I would call the station seven days a week from June through August. I would give a 15-minute rundown on what was happening with the fishery:
- what level the escapement was at,
- where the weak points were,
- what I had planned for openings and closures.

In this way, the fisherman knew what to expect throughout the whole program. There wasn't a commercial fisherman in Cook Inlet who didn't listen to that program during those years. It made a big difference. I had the support of the commercial fisherman.

Jim still confronted (and converted) notorious "creek robbers," i.e., commercial fishermen who routinely violated the regulations.

One of the fisherman was well known for his ability to fish in the creek mouths, which was illegal. I was on a stream survey flight and saw that one of the streams was plugged with pink salmon. This guy's boat was anchored nearby. I knew that as soon as it was dark, he was going to hit that stream. We had more fish than we needed in the stream, so I landed and pulled the "No Fishing" markers. The fisherman came roaring up in a skiff and said, "Who are you? What are you doing?"

I knew who he was. I said, "Help yourself."

He said, "What do you mean, help myself?"

I said, "The stream is open. Just don't go up the creek. We need the spawners."

He said, "Honest to God?"

At the end of the season I had a phone call from this guy. He said, "This is the first year I've ever fished legally throughout the whole season and it's the best year I've ever had."

There was another poacher who was famed for hitting the streams illegally. He was on the outer Kenai Peninsula coast and passed a stream which had a small run of red salmon. There was a big school of salmon trying to get in the stream but there was a log-jam and the fish couldn't get through. He called me on the radio and told me about the log-jam. He says, "I'll stay here and guard these fish until you can get a crew here to clear the log-jam." I sent a couple guys down there with a chain saw. They cleaned it out in short time and the fish ran up. That phone call would never had happened under federal management. That was the kind of mutual respect we developed and allowed us to work together.

Jim innovated the use of sonar to count migrating salmon, replacing the old system of counting "jumpers" and extrapolating. Sonar became the standard method for estimating the size of salmon runs and changed the whole industry.

Cook Inlet has a lot of silty streams. Trying to get escapement figures was almost impossible. They had been using a fish wheel or a gill net or a seine. Some of the cannery superintendents would count the number of jumpers they saw in ten minutes and report that as an indication of the abundance of fish. It meant nothing. During World War II, I was trained as a sonar operator. I spoke with the Commissioner and suggested the fish could be counted with sonar. He gave approval to pursue the concept. I wrote to every sonar company in the United States.

Bendix sent a fellow up here who was an electronics genius. There weren't any salmon running when he was here, but we devised a method to assess the system. He set up his equipment in the Kasilof River. One of my guys put some dead silvers on a line and dragged them in front of the sonar counter. They simulated live fish very well. The sonar picked them up. Within a few years, sonar had become the standard method of counting fish. If I'm going to brag a little bit, that's the thing I'm most proud of.

Jim believed in using biology and science to support management of commercial fisheries. One decision he made on that basis opened up numerous questions.

I made one decision that I'm not sure to this day whether it was a mistake or not. Fishing was open three days a week for a 12-hour period. On a Wednesday, we had fish coming out of our ears. The tenders were all loaded, the fisherman were loaded, our escapement figures were way up. There was no biological reason to close at the end of that 12-hour period. I went on the radio and extended it for another 12 hours. WOW … talk about pandemonium. One of the tenders got on the radio and said, "Now what the hell do we do??" His ship was loaded. I've often thought that I probably should have given them a 12-hour closed period to get caught up and then open it again. We decided we were managing the fishery based on biologic principles and why not leave it open. It's kind of a philosophical question.

Jim flew many hours of stream surveys in the back seat of a Super Cub. He had a couple of close calls in the small, single-engine aircraft.

One day in the 1960s, we were headed to the southeast portion of the Kenai Peninsula. We flew one river from the headwaters down to the mouth. We finished the survey and were coming into Seldovia Bay. The pilot was adjusting the throttle when the throttle control fell off the carburetor and the engine was at an idle. Luckily, here was a big bay in front of us. He made a standard landing, slowly taxied up to the floats in the Seldovia harbor and called for a mechanic. If that had happened anywhere else, we'd have gone into the trees.

On another occasion, we were landing to take groceries and mail to a stream guard at Point Dick. There's a 300-foot-high knob right next to the stream. It was dead calm. The pilot started to make a landing. We were about 50 feet above the water when we passed that knob. A downdraft came off the knob, hit the right wing, and flipped the airplane so the wings were almost vertical. Of course, we lost altitude and we didn't have much of that to lose. The pilot immediately gave full throttle, kicked left rudder, and threw his stick over. As we returned to level flight, the wing tip brushed the water. Neither of us said a word right then, but the minute we landed the pilot said, "You will never … NEVER … come closer than we just did."

One of the hazards in the early years was the state's policy of putting contracts out for bid. We often ended up flying with the guy who bid the lowest. Sometimes he was a new pilot. Sometimes he had bad equipment.

One guy we flew with was a heck of a good pilot but he had a little drinking problem. I'd flown with him quite a bit and I liked him. He got the contract one year. I looked him up and we had a little chat. I said, "If I smell booze on your breath once this season, whether we are flying or if I run into you in town, that's the end of the contract." To my knowledge, he didn't drink a drop all summer.

That New Year's Eve, my wife and I were at the Homestead Restaurant. I was having a drink and all of a sudden there's another drink in front of me. Pretty quick, there's another one and another one! I couldn't keep up.

Finally, I grabbed the bartender and asked, "Where the heck are those coming from." He pointed across to the room at this pilot. He yells back at me, "You kept me sober all summer and now you're going to join me in having some fun!!"

Jim's position as the Outdoor Editor for "Alaska Magazine" was only one of the two major changes that occurred at the end of the decade. Shortly after Jim resigned his job with the state, Governor Bill Egan called and asked if he'd accept a position on the Board of Fish & Game. The former position allowed Jim to make a living. The latter gave him a forum to implement two major changes to wildlife management in the State. During his limited free time, Jim continued to write. His dedication to outdoor writing brought an unexpected opportunity.

I had been writing all these years, weekends and evenings, and was in touch with a lot of magazines. I'd done a lot of writing for the "Alaska Sportsman magazine. Out of nowhere, the owner wrote to me and asked if I'd do some editing for him. I agreed. Next thing I knew, a box with at least 50 manuscripts showed up. He said, "Accept those that are worth publishing. Return all the others. Charge me by the hour, whatever you're worth." So I started. Within a short time, he offered me a full-time salaried job as Outdoor Editor. I accepted and kept that position for 20 years. Those were really interesting years for me.

One of the nice things about having taught at the University and then working for the state was that when I got into writing and editing for "Alaska" magazine, I had good rapport with various biologists around the state.

One time, the head guy at "Alaska" magazine wanted me to go up on the Yukon Flats and get a story of Natives hunting muskrats. He put me in contact with a guy from Fort Yukon. I called this guy and he invited me to his camp up on Beaver Creek. I flew up and camped with him. It was like being in a camp with a bandit. There were guns everywhere. Any time an animal wandered by, the lead would fly. He shot five black bears in the couple of weeks before I got there. The day I arrived, he had killed a cow moose. Here I am, on the Board of Game and I'm eating an illegal cow moose. They had a bunch of kids and they were learning from this guy.

When my chartered plane arrived, he went back to Fairbanks with me. After we got to town, I said, "I want to make something very clear with you. I'm a member of the Board of Game (boy, that Indian turned pale). You invited me to your camp and I was there as a writer to do my job. I want you to know I don't approve of your lifestyle. You claim to be a conservationist, but you're not. You're not following the laws. You're not teaching those kids the proper way to approach life in the Bush." Years later, we were both at a meeting. He kept eyeballing me, afraid I'd spill the beans on him!

That was a real honor. At the first meeting, I questioned the $50 bounty for wolves. I argued that bounties were a waste of money. There's a lot of fraud, and it didn't accomplish anything biologically. I got eight votes and got rid of the bounty on wolves in Alaska.

I had one other major accomplishment. It took several years to get this one approved. I proposed that hunting not be allowed the same day you were airborne. The first time I proposed it, they laughed at me. The second year, they thought "maybe." It took me three or four years before it was passed. It's still in effect and I think most people support it. I think it's worked pretty well.

Over the years, Rearden has become the dean of Alaska outdoor authors. He has expanded from magazine articles to books. His biographies of Sidney Huntington, Frank Glaser, Sam White and Slim Moore are masterpieces of their genre. He is grateful to the people and wildlife of The Great Land, which gave him ample opportunities (both personal and professional).

In summary, Alaska has been really good to me. I couldn't have chosen a better place to live. The challenges were the kind that I loved. The people and the land, have become MY people and MY land.

The professional background I had in wildlife, the self-taught writing, the work with teaching wildlife management, and the people I got to work with were just the greatest. I no longer write magazine articles. I spend my time writing books. I'm up to 18 and working on my nineteenth. I'm perfectly content right here in Homer and I'm very thankful for the life I've had in Alaska.

About the Author

Randy Zarnke was born and raised in Wisconsin. He has hunted and fished most of his life. He moved to Alaska in 1978 following completion of graduate school, and began trapping shortly thereafter. Zarnke worked for the Alaska Department of Fish & Game in Fairbanks as a wildlife disease and parasite specialist for nearly 24 years before retiring in 2002. He has been an active member of the Alaska Trappers Association for decades, and served as ATA President from 2006-11.

"The primary reason I retired from ADF&G was to dedicate more time to this oral history project. I firmly believe in the significance of preserving these memories. In addition, I thoroughly enjoy working with these veteran trappers and hunters. As a result, this project offers the best of two worlds ... it is both rewarding and enjoyable. I hope interested individuals will obtain copies of our audio CDs. Listening to these recordings while driving down the road or sitting around the cabin can provide many hours of entertainment."

> *Full-length audio interviews ranging in length from 30 to 80 minutes are available. You can listen to the unique vocal flavorings of the characters in this book as well as many other Alaskans. More information is available online at: www.alaskatrappers.org. Click on "oral history interviews."*

ALASKA TRACKS

www.ingramcontent.com/pod-product-compliance
Lightning Source LLC
Chambersburg PA
CBHW061257110426
42742CB00012BA/1952